# EQUICIZE

Also by Sally Batton and
Christina Keim:

*The Athletic Equestrian*

# EQUICIZE

**Progressive, Mounted Exercises
That Improve Cardiovascular
and Muscular Fitness for
Everyday Riders of All Levels**

## SALLY BATTON

**and Christina Keim**

Photographs by Ashley Yeaton | Videos by Worthy Gardner

Trafalgar Square
North Pomfret, Vermont

First published in 2024 by
Trafalgar Square Books
North Pomfret, Vermont 05053



**Disclaimer of Liability**
The author and publisher shall have neither liability nor responsibility to any person or entity with respect to any loss or damage caused or alleged to be caused directly or indirectly by the information contained in this book. While the book is as accurate as the author can make it, there may be errors, omissions, and inaccuracies.

Trafalgar Square Books encourages the use of approved safety helmets in all equestrian sports and activities.

Trafalgar Square Books certifies that the content in this book was generated by a human expert on the subject, and the content was edited, fact-checked, and proofread by human publishing specialists with a lifetime of equestrian knowledge. TSB does not publish books generated by artificial intelligence (AI).

**Library of Congress Cataloging-in-Publication Data**
Names: Batton, Sally, author. | Keim, Christina, author.
Title: Equicize : progressive, mounted exercises that improve cardiovascular and muscular fitness for everyday riders of all levels / Sally Batton and Christina Keim.
Description: North Pomfret, Vermont : Trafalgar Square Books, 2024. | Includes index.
Identifiers: LCCN 2023043532 (print) | LCCN 2023043533 (ebook) | ISBN 9781646011964 (paperback) | ISBN 9781646011971 (epub)
Subjects: LCSH: Horsemanship. | Horse sports. | Horses--Training. | Horsemen and horsewomen--Health and hygiene. | Physical fitness--Popular works.
Classification: LCC SF309 .B3333 2022 (print) | LCC SF309 (ebook) | DDC 798.2--dc23/eng/20231109
LC record available at https://lccn.loc.gov/2023043532
LC ebook record available at https://lccn.loc.gov/2023043533

Photographs by Ashley Yeaton
Videos by Worthy Gardner
Book design by Lauryl Eddlemon
Cover design by RM Didier

Printed in China

10 9 8 7 6 5 4 3 2 1

*This book is dedicated to my children*

*Emma, Jenna, and Jack*

# Contents

## PART IV: MOUNTED EQUICIZE ROUTINE   63

## 5: Mounted Equicize Warm-Up   64



## 6: Leg Builders   76



## 7: Balance Challenges   89

101

133

# PART I

# What Is Equicize and What Can It Do for Me?

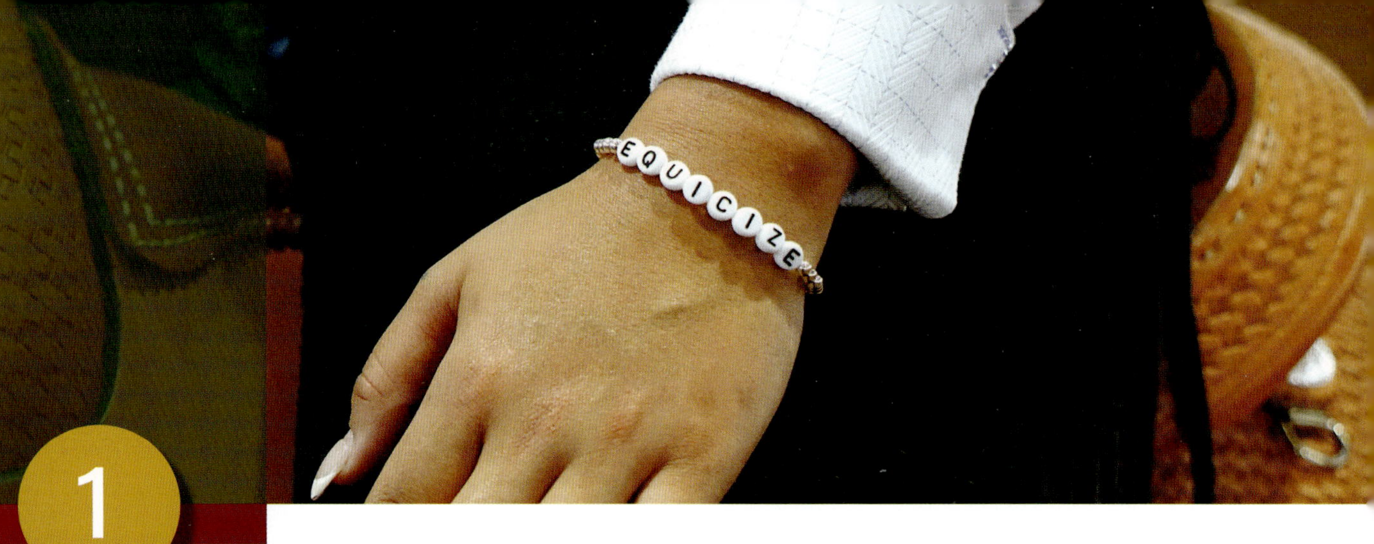



# An Introduction to
# **Equicize**

Ten years ago, I was teaching collegiate varsity riders at Dartmouth College in New Hampshire (fig 1.1). My riders only had 45 minutes of mounted practice in each session, so they would get right to riding without doing any mounted warm-up or conditioning for their bodies beforehand. By most standards, these riders were fit. In addition to their mounted sessions, as members of a varsity team, they were required to complete regular weight-lifting sessions in the gym with a certified trainer, and each week, attend a yoga mobility class as well as a cardio workout like Pilates or spinning. But despite all these workouts, my athletes were not really fit to ride at the level they wanted.

At the same time, the Dartmouth Equestrian Center was home to a robust community riding program, which included many recreation-focused amateur adults. While these riders had very different goals for their riding than my varsity athletes, they had two important qualities in common: first, they desperately wanted to improve their skills and second, they had only a limited amount of time available to ride.

Although I was familiar with many unmounted workout programs, most were not equestrian-specific, and none targeted mounted riders. I began

*Scan to View Video*

studying the exercises my athletes practiced in the varsity gym, as well as those in my own fitness classes (fig. 1.2). I started to wonder if there was a way I could modify these cardio-boosting, muscle-building exercises to be used on horseback. Before I knew it, Equicize was born.

Equicize is a unique series of progressive, mounted exercises that will improve cardiovascular and muscular fitness for "Everyday Riders"—of all levels. Equicize can be used as part of a rider's daily warm-up by targeting specific muscle groups, or for a more intense workout once or twice a week, it can make up the bulk of a training session. No matter your current level of fitness or preferred equestrian discipline, Equicize can help you become the best athlete you can be.

Now, I know what you might be thinking. "Coach Sally, I love this idea but I am too busy to fit one more thing into my schedule. Besides, I have tried 'rider-fitness' programs before, and it is just too hard to stick with them."

1.2 | Equicize was born when I wanted to modify regular gym workouts into mounted cardio-boosting, muscle-building exercises.

The good news is that Equicize is easy to pick up and is flexible by design. There are no complicated dance steps or aerobic routines to learn; there is no fancy terminology or special equipment required (fig. 1.3). Thanks to modifiers for each exercise, Everyday Riders of any fitness level can successfully complete the Equicize sequence. Riders can pick and choose exercises addressing their personal "problem areas," or they can dedicate one (or more!) ride per week to performing the entire sequence. There are literally hundreds of ways to adjust, modify, or adapt Equicize to suit your particular circumstances. In this book, I will offer you several ideas to get started on your personal path to success.

Equicize is accessible to everyone. No matter what level of fitness she starts at, every rider will see improvement in her balance, strength, coordination, and flexibility by practicing the Equicize system regularly. Because adult amateurs lead full, complex lives, Equicize is designed to fit seamlessly into grooming, tacking, and riding time. I have taught hundreds of students these exercises, and they have found it shockingly easy to incorporate Equicize into their regular practice.

*Equicize: Progressive, Mounted Exercises That Improve Cardiovascular and Muscular Fitness for Everyday Riders of All Levels* is your step-by-step guide to mastering the Equicize program. I recommend reviewing the entire book before attempting any of the exercises, then choosing one of three formats to get started: Target Practice, Equicize Lite, or the full Equicize sequence.

Target Practice: Each chapter of this book focuses on a specific area of the rider's body. In Target Practice, the Everyday Rider chooses one area of the body to target and completes those Equicize exercises during her horse's walking warm-up. The next day, she chooses a different region of the body, and completes those exercises. She

should continue through each group of exercises until she has completed them all. As she gains fitness, the rider may choose to add the "upward modifiers" discussed for each exercise, which will increase the intensity of the workout. Target Practice allows riders to multitask by using their horse's warm-up to build their own fitness, while leaving the bulk of their riding time free to focus on other horsemanship skills.

Equicize Lite: This is a modified version of the full program, touching on all the major body regions, without going into as much depth or intensity as the full workout. Equicize Lite is a great option if you want to do more than just a few specific exercises in warm-up, but you also want to use some of your schooling session to work on other skills (see Appendix B, p. 145).

Full Equicize Sequence: Complete the Full Equicize Sequence, dedicating an entire riding session to building your personal strength and fitness. This is a great starting point if you already consider yourself to be a fairly fit rider-athlete and want to have a solid baseline from which to set goals for future workouts. But thanks to the modifiers included for each exercise, anyone can tackle the full sequence simply by choosing the variation that best suits their current level of experience and fitness.

Because I cannot be there ringside to coach you through this process, I have provided the next best thing—photos and videos of each exercise, demonstrated by Everyday Riders. Just scan the QR codes you'll see throughout these pages with your smart phone for a quick visual tutorial of each exercise in action.

Most riders spend more time out of the tack than in it. As an added bonus, throughout this book are Everyday Equicize sidebars, which detail easy unmounted exercises Everyday Riders can do at home, at work, or even while waiting in line (fig. 1.4). By

1.5 | In order to stay focused on your Equicize routine, you'll find Gold, Silver and Bronze checklists to help you track your progress at the back of the book on page 147.

incorporating Everyday Equicize into her daily routine, a rider is certain to notice a positive improvement in muscle tone, coordination, and elasticity during her mounted work.

When it comes to our personal fitness, the truth is that most of us are so busy with work, our horses, and our families that it can be hard to stay self-motivated when it comes to completing exercise routines. To help you stay on task with your Equicize journey, in this book you will find Bronze, Silver, and Gold checklists in Appendix C (p. 147) to help you track your progress (fig. 1.5). As you grow increasingly fit and reach defined thresholds for each set of exercises, you will earn not only bragging rights but the opportunity to order a corresponding bracelet from my Equicize.com website to commemorate your achievement (fig. 1.6).

I hope you can see that Equicize is a doable, adaptable fitness system, custom-built for Everyday Riders—riders just like you.

1.6 | As you reach defined thresholds for each checklist you can show off your accomplishments by ordering a bracelet at equicize.com to commemorate your achievement.

# PART II

# Equicize Essentials

2

# Equicize Essentials

Before we get into the nuts and bolts of what Equicize looks like in practice, I want to discuss several important logistical details. Some of these points are more relevant for riders using Equicize, while others are more important for instructors teaching it. However, to ensure success for all parties, I encourage all readers to review the entire list before getting started.

## REQUIRED RIDING SKILLS

Although the Equicize system will benefit riders regardless of preferred discipline or experience level, a rider at the very beginning of her horsemanship journey may need to develop her foundation skills prior to attempting Equicize. At a minimum, riders need to confidently and independently perform the rising trot while maintaining basic control of their mount. Even though we do not use the canter during Equicize, it can also be helpful for riders to have at least basic experience with this gait. Learning to follow the canter builds a rider's confidence, challenges her balance, and begins to tone her core—all qualities that will help her during Equicize.

The majority of Equicize exercises are practiced at the rising trot, even when the rider is using a Western saddle. In general, I do not recommend practicing Equicize in the sitting trot. It is simply too much for the rider to coordinate, and therefore potentially stressful for the horse. However, for riders more accustomed to sitting to the trot (for example, Western or dressage riders), a handful of exercises may be performed in this gait variation for added challenge.

## REQUIRED EQUIPMENT AND ATTIRE

In chapter 1, I told you that Equicize doesn't require any special equipment—and this is still true. However, in working with hundreds of riders, I have learned that certain types of equipment and attire can make Equicize more accessible.

*Scan to View Video*

### Saddles

When I first started teaching Equicize, I thought the system would only work in an English-type saddle. Over the years, I have learned how to modify certain exercises to suit a wider range of disciplines, and today I regularly do Equicize with riders in hunter seat, dressage, Western, and even saddleseat saddles (figs. 2.1 A–C). The most

**2.1 A | Equicize can be performed in a hunter seat type saddle.**

**2.1 B | In a dressage saddle, typically with a shorter stirrup.**

significant modification will be for those riders accustomed to using a longer stirrup, because Equicize requires riders to use the two-point position. Regardless of their saddle style, riders will need to shorten their stirrups until there is a soft bend in the knee, allowing them to comfortably balance with their seat both out of the saddle and positioned over the horse's center.

## Reins

There are several Equicize exercises in which the rider starts with both reins in one hand, and then needs to smoothly transition them into the other. To facilitate this process, I usually shorten the reins to the location on the horse's neck where the rider's hand is positioned in two-point, and tie them in a knot (fig. 2.2A). This keeps the reins out of the way without risk of them sliding around, while leaving them within easy reach should it be necessary to grab them.

*Scan to View Video*

2.2 A | Many Equicize exercises require both reins in one hand. One way to facilitate this is to shorten your reins and tie them in a knot.

2.2 B | Another option to hold your reins in one hand is to bridge your reins. To bridge your reins, take each rein across the horse's neck and hold it with the opposite hand. Once you have made the "bridge," you can transfer it into one hand which frees up the other hand and arm to do the Equicize arm exercises.

2.2 C | I love using the Correct Connect Aaron Vale reins for one-handed Equicize. They feature hand grips that not only make holding the reins easier but make transferring them into one hand a breeze.

Another option is to teach riders how to bridge their reins, taking each rein across the horse's neck and holding it with the opposite hand (fig. 2.2 B). For bridged reins to work effectively in this circumstance, the length of the bridge should be no more than 6 to 8 inches between the rider's hands.

More recently, I have experienced great success with the Correct Connect™ Aaron Vale reins (fig. 2.2 C). These specialized reins feature a padded grip, similar to a rein stop, that makes not only holding onto the rein but transferring it from one hand to the other easy. Sometimes, when

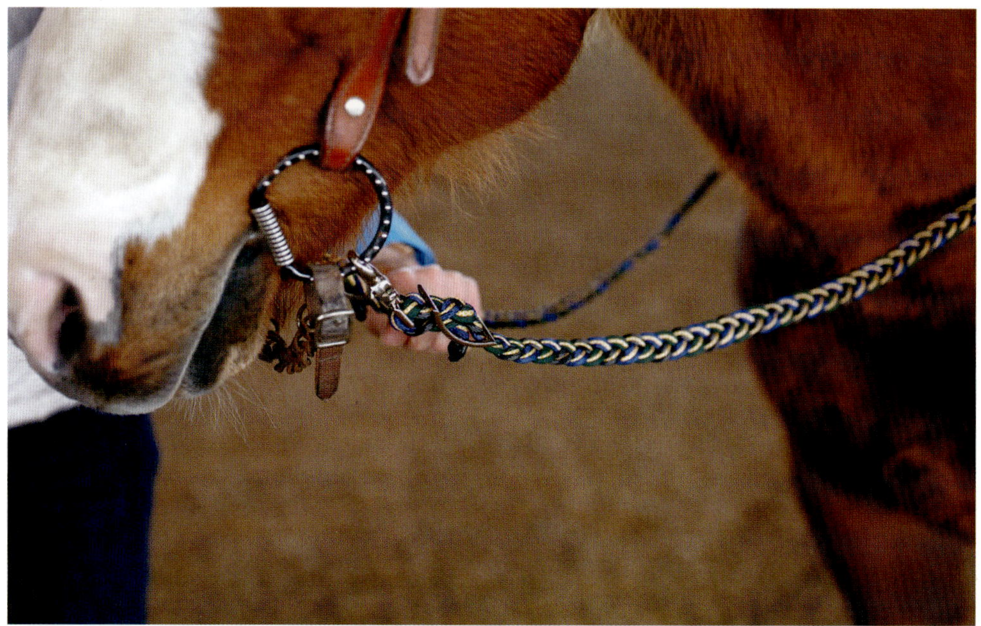

2.3 A | Many Equicize riders enjoy using gaming-type reins that clip onto the bit and are made with easy-to-hold paracord. These reins are sold through Reins for Rescues and the sales go toward supporting the rescue horses at Triple Dream Farm.

a rider is concentrating on the movement she is performing, she can inadvertently loosen her grip on the reins, and the next thing you know, she is no longer steering her horse. The padded grips of the Correct Connect reins help riders to retain control even if their fingers open slightly while performing an exercise.

Finally, some riders have found the gaming-style reins popular with Western and endurance riders to be a great alternative to traditional leather reins. One style I particularly like is made by Reins for Rescues: their adjustable reins clip to the bit and are made with several woven strands of soft, easy-to-hold paracord (fig. 2.3 A). If needed, riders can easily tie knots in the reins for custom "grip" points, and the generally shorter rein length keeps them more centered and stable over the horse's neck when the rider lets go with one hand. In addition, the reins come in many fun colors and proceeds from their sale go toward supporting the rescue horses at Triple Dream Farm—a win in my book!

Another style I like are the BioThane® reins made by Color Up Pet—like the woven reins, BioThane comes in many fun colors and can add a splash to your Equicize attire (fig. 2.3 B).

If you regularly ride in a type of bit that requires two sets of reins, I recommend you either switch to a plain snaffle for Equicize or simply tie your second rein in a knot and not use it.

## Riding Attire

Because of the range of movement required in Equicize, riders will be most comfortable wearing layered, close-fitting attire, similar to what you would choose to wear during a routine ride. I guarantee when you do Equicize, you are going to sweat, so when you are riding in cooler temperatures, layers are a must!

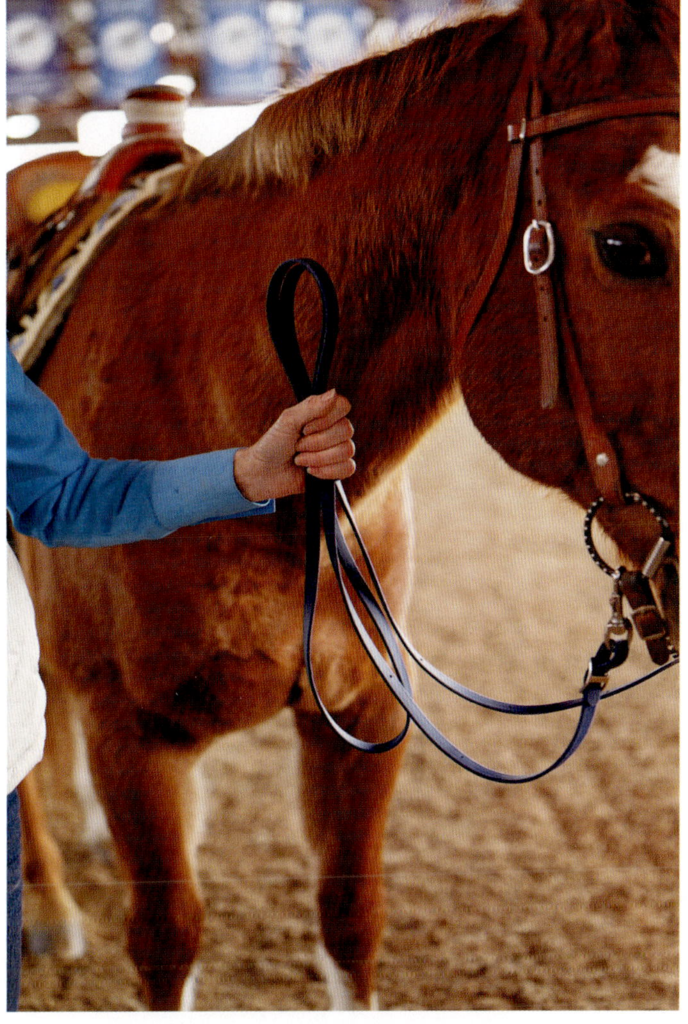

For English-discipline riders, I prefer paddock boots with half chaps to leather tall boots (though it is certainly possible to do the exercises in tall boots if that is your preferred footwear). In my experience, half chaps allow for more flexibility in the rider's movement than tall boots, and are less likely to cause a pinch behind the knee or at the ankle while doing Equicize. Remember, when you are doing these exercises, you will be moving and holding your body in postures that are quite different from your typical riding position (fig. 2.4).

2.4 | Half chaps and paddock boots allow for more flexibility during your Equicize workout than breeches and tall boots. Tall boots can be worn but when doing these exercises you will be moving and holding your body in postures that are different from your usual riding position.

2.5 | Western riders can perform Equicize in their typical cowboy boots and jeans. A word of caution: you may want to leave your chunky belt buckle at home because it can get in the way of your exercises.

2.6 | Riding sneakers allow more flexibility at the ankle than a paddock or cowboy boot—and they can help put riders in the mindset of working out.

2.7 | Jodhpur clips work great to help keep pant legs securely down, which minimizes the risk of chafe.

Western riders may practice Equicize in their typical cowboy boots and jeans, but leave your big, chunky belt buckle at home—it will definitely get in the way (fig. 2.5)! Choose a more modest-sized belt buckle on Equicize days instead.

*Scan to View Video*

Riders from all disciplines might find that riding sneakers are more comfortable to wear with your half chaps or jeans. Riding sneakers tend to allow greater flexibility in the rider's ankle than traditional boots, which can be a real help when doing Equicize. Several manufacturers offer variations of this product, and as they come in traditional colors like black or brown, they blend well with the rest of a rider's attire (fig. 2.6).

Additionally, riders choosing long pants and low boots might appreciate a pair of jodhpur clips to help keep the pant leg down where it belongs (fig. 2.7). Usually made of a sturdy elastic and adorned with two simple clips at either end, jodhpur clips can attach to any pant without damaging it and will prevent the fabric from sliding, creeping up the leg, or bunching, any of which can cause painful chafing and rubs.

Finally, regardless of discipline, all riders should be wearing a well-fitting riding helmet certified to the current ASTM/SEI standard.

## Arm Weights

All Equicize exercises have modifiers to make them slightly easier or more challenging, depending on the rider's needs. When first becoming familiar with the exercises, most riders notice muscular fatigue immediately or sometimes the following day. As with any exercise program, the more frequently Equicize is performed to a particular

*Scan to View Video*

degree of intensity and duration, the more comfortable the athlete will feel as her body adjusts to the work. This is also a good sign that her body is ready to increase the challenge.

One easy way to add intensity to the arm exercises in Equicize is to use 1- or 2-pound runner's arm weights (fig. 2.8). These come in a variety of styles, but for Equicize, I prefer the version that attaches to the wrist with a Velcro

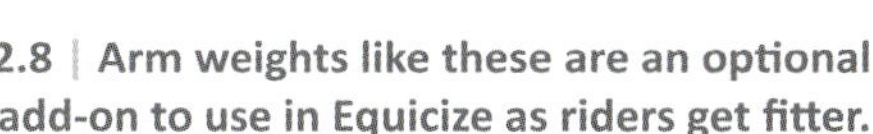

2.8 | Arm weights like these are an optional add-on to use in Equicize as riders get fitter.

strap. I will go into more detail regarding the use of these weights in chapter 8 (p. 104).

## Arm Bands

Even after you are familiar with the Equicize exercises, it can be challenging to remember all of them, in order, once you are in the ring. This is true whether you are teaching Equicize to others or practicing the exercises yourself. Although you can certainly leave this book ringside, or copy the lists I have provided detailing the full sequence (Appendix A, p. 143) or Equicize Lite (Appendix B, p. 145), I have another solution to offer you.

When I teach clinics, I write down the exercises I plan to teach on a card and slide it into an arm band (fig. 2.9). I wear the arm band on my biceps where it is easy for me to glance down to make sure I am staying on track with my clinic plan. The arm band is easily adjustable and so light I don't even notice I'm wearing it. You can order yours from www.equicize.com.

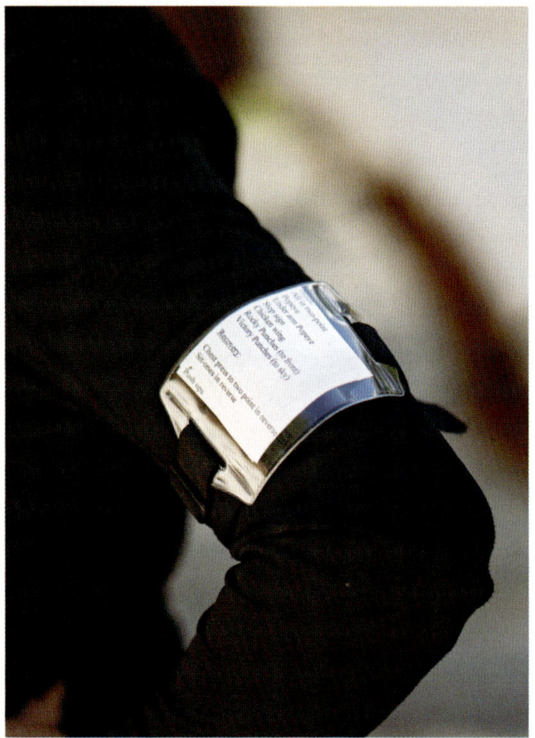

2.9 | Riders and instructors alike can keep track of which workout they are doing by using a clear plastic sleeve on their upper arm for easy reference.

## EQUINE REQUIREMENTS

In general, nearly any horse can make a suitable Equicize mount. I have coached riders on everything from Haflingers to paints, draft crosses to Appaloosas, and all these wonderful animals have been successful Equicize partners (fig. 2.10). In general, I don't exclude any horse from being an Equicize mount based on breed or age alone.

With that being said, some horses do find the unusual movements of the rider during Equicize to be unsettling, and they can respond accordingly. This might look like an increase of speed within the trot, a spontaneous transition to canter, or confusion regarding the rider's steering aids as she navigates riding one-handed while balancing in two-point and performing an arm exercise. Most often, experienced mounts simply need a few repetitions to get used to the rider's unfamiliar movement, and return to their typical steady performance.

For horses that still seem unsettled after some practice, I will try modifying exercises slightly to see if this helps restore the animal's equilibrium. Usually, this looks like taking more time between the movements in each exercise. For example, in the Sit-One Sequence (see p. 73), I might have the rider spread out the timing so she is sitting once every eight or ten strides, instead of once every five. If loss of steering is an issue when a rider does her Toe Touches (p. 93) to the inside leg, I have her try only reaching toward her outside toe, then I ask her to change directions to get the same stretch on the other side of her body.

Of all the Equicize exercises, it is perhaps the Chest Press (p. 78) that can elicit the most concern from the horse. When a horse is coping well with all other exercises but speeds up whenever the rider goes into this deep two-point position, I modify so the position is held for a shorter period of time, or I have the rider take a few laps of rising trot in between her Chest Press sets to allow the horse to regroup.

Do use good judgment and horsemanship skills when assessing your mount for Equicize suitability. This is probably not the right job for a horse newly started under saddle or fresh off the racetrack. If you are not sure if your horse is a good match, check in with a qualified equine professional for advice.

## The Walk Break: A Tale of Two Functions

Throughout this book, I regularly remind you that any Equicize exercise can be performed at the halt, walk, or trot. It is up to each of you, as an individual, to assess how easy or difficult a given exercise feels, then choose the modification that pushes you to your personal edge. Your edge is the place at which you feel the effort an exercise requires, but it does not feel impossible to perform. When you are practicing an exercise at your edge, you can still maintain a steady breath, and do not experience pain.

As an Everyday Rider works to master the mechanics required for each exercise, she may find she becomes fatigued to the point that she requires a short walk break to relieve shaking muscles or to restore a steady flow to her breath. Sometimes this is a sign she has pushed beyond her edge, or that she is concentrating so hard she has forgotten to breathe. It can also just be a normal part of developing increased fitness. After the Everyday Rider has taken a moment to reset by sitting in a neutral balance at the walk while restoring her breath, she should resume the exercise from the point where she left off. It is advisable to perhaps back off slightly in the intensity, so she does not again push to the point where she needs a walk break to recover.

# ADVICE FOR INSTRUCTORS

When I first experimented with the idea of Equicize, it was my adult amateurs who fully embraced it. They loved getting a fitness class in for themselves while also riding and catching up with friends. Some even chose to add a second lesson to their routine; one lesson was dedicated to riding technique while the second was entirely focused on Equicize. When Equicize was presented in a group lesson, students encouraged and supported each other through the challenge of each exercise—and that, in turn, helped maintain motivation and commitment to the process.

But Equicize works equally well in a one-on-one setting, particularly if you have the luxury of offering longe lessons. The longe line takes away any concerns the rider

As Everyday Riders grow fitter, demonstrated by the ability to perform an increasing percentage of the Equicize sequence at the trot (whether posting or in two-point), it grows increasingly important that they are also mindful of their equine partners. Depending on a rider's mount's age, breed, soundness, and overall condition, it might be necessary to take a walk break—not for the rider's sake, but for her horse. When an Everyday Rider is not sure how to assess her horse's level of fitness or is not aware of signs that a horse could require a walk break, she should check with an experienced equine professional for advice.

But in Equicize, if you are walking because your horse needs a break, it doesn't mean you get one as well! If you are working through the Equicize sequence but need to return to the walk while your mount catches his breath on a long rein, keep your own physical and mental effort up by getting into your two-point position, holding it for as long as is necessary for your horse to recover.

The most advanced modification in this situation is to practice your two-point without stirrups. It takes quite a bit of practice to get strong enough to do this for more than a few strides in a row, but you have to start somewhere! Using the strength of your legs, hold your two-point until you find your edge, then with control, return to the saddle. Breathe for a beat or two, then try again, repeating it until your horse is recovered enough to resume the trot.

2.11 | Equicize is usually done in groups but works equally well in a one-on-one setting, particularly if you have the luxury of longe lessons.

might have about steering or otherwise staying in control of her mount. Whether she is a newer rider working on her balance while doing the baseline Equicize sequence, or a more experienced rider trying the program without stirrups for the first time, longeing can be an invaluable tool (fig. 2.11).

If you are teaching Equicize in a group, there are really two "best practice" methods of managing the arena: riders can spread themselves out around the ring and maintain a safe distance from other horses (fig. 2.12 A), or they can ride in a nose-to-tail file with just a single horse length's distance from the mount ahead of them (fig. 2.12 B). Which method you choose will depend on the horses you are using; we all have that one lesson horse that goes much faster (or slower) than the rest!

I have had equal success teaching Equicize while standing in the middle of the arena or while mounted on a horse. In either case, I actively demonstrate each

2.12 A & B | To manage the arena, riders can spread out around the ring and maintain a safe distance from other horses (A). Another way to manage the arena is to ride nose-to-tail with just a single horse length's distance from the mount ahead. Equicize riders practice their two-point without stirrups at a clinic at Equine Affaire in Springfield, Massachusetts (B).

2.13 A & B | You can teach Equicize standing in the middle of the arena and demonstrating the movements while keeping count as I'm doing here (A). Another way to teach Equicize is while mounted. Here, Megan at Turning Point Show Stables in East Kingston, New Hampshire, wears a WinBridge Voice amplifier on her belt while leading a class (B).

exercise that I am teaching, and I will help riders to keep moving in a steady rhythm through a verbal count. You could find this easier to do with a voice amplifier (I like the WinBridge Voice Amplifier), particularly when you are mounted and riding at the head of the line (figs. 2.13 A & B).

## MUSIC

Whether you are practicing Equicize solo or as part of a group, music is a must. Make a playlist of your favorite songs with a strong, steady "one-two" beat and play it either through ear buds or over a speaker. Music helps Equicizers stay in rhythm and distracts them from the effort or discomfort that pushing their body physically can cause—plus, it makes the ride more fun!

# A FEW NOTES ON INCREASING CHALLENGE

When a rider first starts using Equicize, almost every exercise will cause her to feel the effort through increased heart and respiratory rates. She won't need a FitBit® or other device to know the work is increasing her cardiovascular output—her sweat and faster breathing will be proof enough! It is also common for riders to become winded and need a walk break to catch their breath.

However, as a rider gets into the routine of using Equicize during her rides, she should gain both strength and endurance. She may notice she no longer needs as many (or any) walk breaks, or that her muscles are no longer sore after doing the work.

When exercises start to feel easy, it is time to increase the difficulty. In simple terms, exercises can be made more difficult through increasing intensity or duration. Depending on the exercise, this can be achieved by increasing the number of repetitions or applying modifiers such as adding two-point or dropping the stirrups. In the

*Scan to View Video*

2.14 | To increase the difficulty of Equicize, riders can make all the exercises more difficult by adding the two-point or dropping their stirrups.

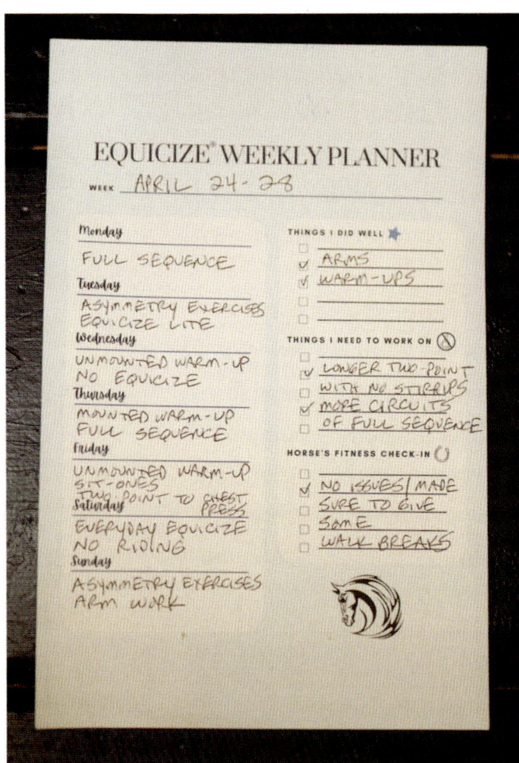


**2.15 | Keep a riding log and record the exercises completed, the number of repetitions or count achieved, and a few notes about how your body felt both during the exercise and after the ride was over. The Equicize planners are available for purchase at www.equicize.com.**

chapters to follow, I will detail the modifiers for each exercise and offer recommendations as to their implementation (fig 2.14).

I strongly recommend that riders keep a riding log or daily diary of their Equicize progress. Record the exercises completed, the number of repetitions or count achieved, and a few notes about how your body felt both during the exercise and after the ride was over (fig. 2.15).

Every rider will have her own goals for Equicize, and those goals often change over time. You may start with the objective of completing the full Equicize sequence at the trot with some two-point, which can build to doing the entire sequence (including arm exercises) in two-point. Eventually, some riders are able to do portions or the majority of the exercises without stirrups.

What is most important is that the goal each Everyday Rider sets is appropriate for her and her circumstances. Don't compare yourself to your barn friends, your trainer, or even yourself 15 years ago. Instead, focus on the day-to-day improvements, and realize that with each step, you are getting closer to the fittest version of yourself.

# Fundamental Concepts

To successfully implement several elements of the Equicize program, riders must understand and be able to execute the correct biomechanics of the two-point position. Additionally, all Equicizers must be able to utilize their Power Leg (p. 32), a specialized leg position that gives the rider stability and balance.

For readers of my first book, *The Athletic Equestrian*, these concepts will sound familiar because I addressed them there in great detail. In this chapter, I will review these fundamentals, speaking particularly to those riders whose equestrian background has perhaps not included much (or any) work over fences, as jumping is the most common reason for a rider to practice her two-point. But this will also be a helpful review even for those riders who are already familiar with two-point, as it is easy for bad habits to creep into our execution of this commonly used English riding position.

Before we get started, I want to reassure my Western, dressage, saddleseat, and other non-jumping English riders that "YOU CAN DO THIS!" (figs. 3.1 A & B). Although two-point is often referred to as "jumping position" by instructors, you do not need to be a jumping rider to learn how to do it correctly. In Equicize,

3.1 A | Any discipline can perform the two-point position for their Equicize exercises. Athough two-point can also be used for jumping, for our purposes it is used to challenge a rider's balance and improve her overall strength in any type of saddle. Here, Tami demonstrates the two-point in a Western saddle at Dartmouth Riding Center in Etna, New Hampshire.

3.1 B | Reina demonstrates the two-point position in a dressage saddle at Floyd Woods Farm in Lempster, New Hampshire.

two-point is used to challenge a rider's balance (which causes her to engage her core muscles) and to improve her overall strength. In this book, I will only refer to this position as "two-point," and I want you to think of it as an exercise position that you will practice for a specific purpose.

Before tackling any Equicize exercises that use the two-point position, the rider must practice it enough to feel balanced, secure, and safe. Without this solid foundation, riders will feel off-balance and uncomfortable—and they may give up on Equicize unnecessarily.

## TWO-POINT FUNDAMENTALS FOR EQUICIZE

The term "two-point" position comes from the fact that while performing it, the rider has two points of contact on her horse—her legs. In two-point, the rider's seat is totally clear from the saddle, and the angles in her ankles, knees, and hips become more closed than when she is seated or posting. The most extreme example of a two-point is a jockey position, but fortunately you will not need to take it to that level of balance for Equicize!

Two-point is a form of athletic stance, another concept I discuss in more depth in *The Athletic Equestrian.* Athletic stance is a body position utilized in almost every sport. In athletic stance, the athlete is balanced over her feet, with a bend in her ankles and knees and a flexible hip (fig. 3.2). Athletic stance is what allows for the mobility of a tennis player returning a serve, the coiled power

3.2 | Simone demonstrates her athletic stance, a body position utilized in almost every sport. She is balanced over her feet, with a bend in her ankles and knees and a flexible hip.

of a gymnast landing off a vault, or the balance of a surfer riding a wave (fig. 3.3). With bent, flexible joints, an athlete can absorb and store energy, helping her to stay balanced and move fluidly.

When they hear me say that their seat should be out of the saddle in two-point, some riders attempt to achieve this by just standing up straight in their stirrups. While this is a good balance challenge (and we actually utilize a variation of this in Equicize, with the Stand Ones sequence), it is not a correct two-point position. In a biomechanically correct two-point, the rider sinks deeper into her lower leg, increasing the depth of the heel, then lifts her seat out of the saddle and slides her hips back, until her "center" (which is just behind the belly button and about an inch in front of the spine) is over the horse's "center" (fig. 3.4). Her knee remains centered over the ball of her foot, and her stirrup leather is almost perpendicular to the ground.

In two-point, the rider should never be balanced with her seat over the pommel. The good news, at least for Western and dressage riders, is that the design of your saddle will help prevent you from standing straight up. The horn of a Western saddle and higher pommel of a dressage saddle physically interfere if the rider tries to (incorrectly) come into two-point by standing up and leaning forward in the saddle. The flip side, however, is that these same saddle-design features will limit how closed the hip angle can be in two-point as compared to a rider in a jumping saddle. This will slightly affect how riders in these types of saddle will execute the Chest Press, an Equicize exercise that is essentially an extremely deep version of two-point (p. 78). I will explain how to adjust for this in chapter 6 (p. 82).

If you have limited or no experience with two-point, it is important to build a base of fitness in this position before attempting to add Equicize exercises into the

**3.4** | **Amanda demonstrates a correctly balanced two-point with her heel deep and her seat lifted slightly out of the saddle until her center is over the horse's center of balance.**

# The Sally Batton Pommel Blocker by Correct Connect

One of the most common mistakes I see in riders when executing the two-point position is opening the angles in the leg and standing up in the stirrups (fig. 3.5). This brings the rider's upper body up and forward over the pommel, and it is an extremely unbalanced position. In many cases, this error has become engrained into a rider's muscle memory, meaning that no matter how many times her instructor reminds her to change, her brain unconsciously continues to practice this incorrect technique.

In my clinics, I use many what I call "Teaching Tools" to fix common rider problems just like this one. After 35 years of watching riders post too high or stand over their pommel in two-point position, I came up with a simple solution—the Pommel Blocker (fig. 3.6). The Pommel Blocker is a tool that allows a rider to feel when she moves her body up over the pommel, giving her immediate kinesthetic feedback which then allows her to change her biomechanics.

Over the years, my Pommel Blocker went through many variations as I tried to find the perfect combination of materials and attachments. My prototype version was actually a repurposed Halloween costume for a dog! It looked like two frosted donuts connected by a strap to go under the dog's belly; instead, I

3.5 | When a rider opens the angles of her leg and stands in the stirrups in two-point, she is "ahead" of the horse's "center." Not only is the rider extremely unbalanced while in this position, it is uncomfortable for the horse. If you don't believe me, just look at the expression of the horse in this photo!

strapped it to the saddle's D rings with Velcro, and the "donuts" sat over the pommel (fig. 3.7). While I didn't stick with this design, it did show me that the concept had potential to help riders develop a new, more correct, biomechanical habit. In *The Athletic Equestrian,* I teach readers how to make their own Pommel Blocker using a child's inflatable swimming float and a piece of Velcro.

More recently, I have been able to work with the design team at Correct Connect, a company that is among the leaders in developing rider training aids, to create the Sally Batton Pommel Blocker. This Teaching Tool is made of high-quality synthetic leather and attaches to the saddle D-rings with Velcro at the front of the Pommel Blocker. It attaches at

3.6 | After years of watching riders post too high or stand over their pommel in two-point position, I came up with a simple solution—the Pommel Blocker, a tool that allows a rider to feel when she moves her body up over the pommel, giving her immediate kinesthetic feedback, which then allows her to change her biomechanics.

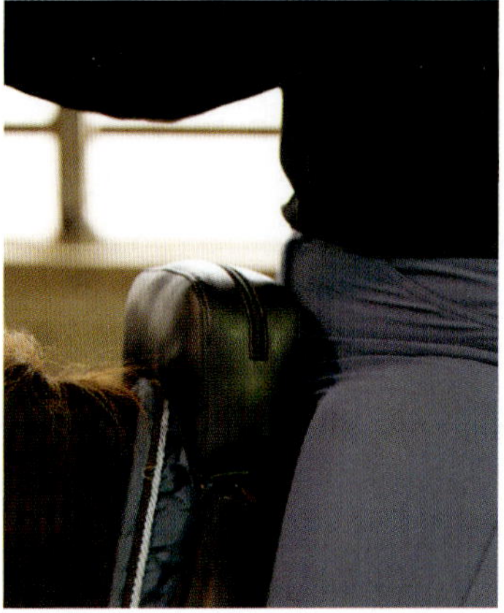

*Scan to View Video*

the back of the Pommel Blocker with a wide, nylon overgirth, which is placed in front of the stirrups and over the horse's girth and pulled snug. With a firm block over the pommel, this tool is the perfect way to retrain your body to move correctly and smoothly into two-point with closed angles and deep heels.

As with all my Training Tools, a Pommel Blocker is not meant to be used forever. I recommend riding with the Pommel Blocker for 15 or 20 minutes of your set, then removing it. Continue your practice, trying to maintain the same position without the Training Tool as you had when using it. This Training Tool gives riders a cue to change how they are holding or using their body—but it is still ultimately up to the rider to work toward a new, corrected kinesthetic awareness that will become her body's new muscle memory.

To learn more about the Sally Batton Pommel Blocker, please scan the QR code.

3.7 | My Pommel Blocker prototype was actually a dog's Halloween costume with frosted doughnuts with Velcro that I attached to the saddle D-rings. Needless to say, this design didn't last long!

mix. Start by shortening your stirrups two, three, or even four holes. They need to be short enough so you can achieve depth in the heel and a more closed knee, which will allow you to lift your pelvis clear of the saddle. Create enough bend in your joints so that should your horse magically disappear out from underneath you, you would land balanced and centered, on your feet, in athletic stance.

When practicing two-point at first, start small—it is a different way of holding your body, and it will take time for the muscles, tendons, and ligaments in your legs to adapt. Start with perhaps half a circuit of the arena, then take a break. Repeat, up to five repetitions. The next day, try for one lap. Continue to check your mechanics: in two-point, you are first sinking down into your leg, then lifting your seat and sliding your hips back. It can be helpful to have a friend take a short video to confirm that you are executing the two-point correctly.

A rider who is well-balanced in two-point should feel fairly stable, but not necessarily at ease—it will take effort to hold this position. If she keeps falling back into the saddle, her lower leg has come too far forward (fig. 3.8 A). If she is tipping forward or catching her balance on the horse's neck, she is probably pinching with her knee, and the lower leg has slid back (fig. 3.8 B). In either case, return to the correct alignment— ear, shoulder, hip, heel—while seated, and focus on holding the lower leg still and in against the horse's side as you transition into two-point.

Make sure you keep your heels lower than your toes. This is easier for some bodies than others, and when riders feel challenged (whether in posting trot or two-point position), they tend to tip onto their toes and lift their heels, resulting in a loss of balance. To help keep the heels down, roll slightly onto the inside ball of the foot; this position allows the heel to stretch to its max. To gain confidence, riders can practice this position in their shorter stirrups before attempting two-point.

## INTRODUCING THE POWER LEG

When riders are practicing their two-point, it is quite common to see their lower legs swinging back and forth, or for the legs to be positioned too far forward or too far back. A lower leg that is out of position for any reason is the number one cause of a rider losing her balance in two-point. But when a rider learns how to use her Power

3.8 A & B | A correct two-point position is essential. When the rider keeps falling back into the saddle, most likely her leg is too far forward. Edie demonstrates this, which causes her seat to be too close to the saddle (A). Edie demonstrates a leg that is pinched at the knee that makes her leg slide too far back which causes her to lose her balance (B). Edie rides for New Hampton Equestrian at Wakewood Farm in Plymouth, New Hampshire.

Leg, her lower leg will stay stable and consistent, making her feel more balanced and ultimately increasing her confidence.

And the best part of all is that Power Leg is so easy to learn!

The Power Leg is perhaps one of the most important concepts I teach riders at my clinics, and for Equicizers, using the Power Leg can make the difference between frustration and success. In the most basic of descriptions, Power Leg is a slight change in the rider's lower leg placement that helps to keep it in position and stable, especially in two-point position. Let me explain.

Think of the lower leg as having three zones:

- Zone 1 is the rider's inner calf, which rests on the horse's side most of the time and is used to create an upward transition (fig. 3.9 A).

- Zone 2 is the rider's upper calf, the broader belly of the muscle (fig. 3.9 B).

- Finally, Zone 3 is the extreme back of the calf. For our purposes, Zone 3 should never be on the horse's side (though there are a few limited circumstances in which this position is used, none of them apply to Equicize).

For most riders, when their leg is resting on the horse's side, Zone 1 is in contact. This position is effective for cueing the horse, but it does not help the rider keep her leg stable while the horse is in motion. But by moving the lower leg forward ever so slightly (not more than one inch, for most riders) and softly rotating the toe externally, the rider can bring Zone 2 into contact—and suddenly, the lower leg is virtually locked into place.

To an observer, the difference between a leg placed on Zone 1 versus Zone 2 is not very apparent. But for the rider, the change is significant; over and over, I have had riders tell me how supported and stable they feel when they use Power Leg. Without Power Leg, riders often resort to using their back muscles and hip flexors to hold their body in two-point, causing stiffness, discomfort, and extreme muscle fatigue. With Power Leg, the rider is able to utilize the full strength of her leg muscles, and she will be able to allow her body to move with the horse.

**3.9 A** | To get a stable and secure lower leg, I teach all my riders the Power Leg. Here the rider's leg is connected to the horse in Zone I, or the inside of the calf. This is the leg position where most riders are accustomed to carrying their calves.

**3.9 B** | Here, the rider has moved her calf to Zone 2, which is the belly of the calf muscle. The rider moves the leg forward ever so slightly and softly rotates the toe externally. This is the Power Leg that gives the rider stability and security in the saddle.

I recommend that riders go out to the rail and experiment with their Power Leg, moving their lower-leg contact on the horse from Zone 1 to Zone 2, to feel the difference. Take it in small chunks, and work to build your endurance in two-point while holding the Zone 2 calf on your horse's side. Eventually, riders should find a "sweet spot" where their seat is centered over their horse's "center," and their leg is firmly in position beneath their hip. This is the place where a rider is truly balanced in two-point.

It is from this dynamic, supported, supple, and balanced position that Equicize exercises like Two-Point to Chest Press, Two-Point Toe Touches, and One-Handed Chest Press can create their maximum effect.

I know you are excited to get started, but I will reiterate here that until you feel strong and confident enough to maintain two-point position for multiple circuits at the walk and trot, don't try to add the Equicize exercises that require two-point just yet. Instead, concentrate on some of the posting exercises—like Sit-Ones, Pommel Stands, or the Gluteal and Abdominal Squeezes—while you build your strength and endurance in two-point.

# PART III

# Grooming Equicize

# Equicize Unmounted Warm-Up:
# Grooming Stretches

In my experience, most riders could benefit from a more thoughtful warm-up—both unmounted and mounted—before their rides. Often, riders are so focused on their horses they forget to consider that they, too, are athletes. To receive the maximum benefit from the Equicize workout, as well as reduce the risk of excessive physical stress, strain, or injury, Everyday Riders must prepare their bodies through a proper warm-up. Being conscious that most Everyday Riders have limited time at the barn, I developed a series of stretches and movements that can be incorporated into your grooming and tack-up routine. If you do these exercises, by the time you mount up, your body will be ready for the work ahead!

Once a rider is comfortable with these Grooming Stretches, I recommend practicing them before every ride, even if Equicize isn't on the agenda for that day's work. Routine stretching keeps soft tissue supple and loose, increases circulation, and improves mobility—all qualities that allow bodies to be strong and resilient when under the stress of work.

Although I have presented the Grooming Stretches in a particular order, in truth, you can do them in most any order that makes sense to you. If you are short on time, you can reduce the number of repetitions for each stretch, or even do certain exercises on alternating days.

## Grooming Stretch #1: Grooming Box Lunge

In the Grooming Box Lunge, the rider will lunge to pick up and replace each grooming tool in her box, alternating the forward leg. For example, if she intends to pick her horse's feet, she will lunge with a bent right knee to pick up the hoof pick, then lunge with a bent left knee to return it.

*Scan to View Video*

To set up, place your grooming box in a location where you can safely perform a lunge without putting your head or legs next to or underneath the horse's belly. Standing about 3 feet away from the grooming box, step forward with the right leg until the tip of your toe touches the tote (fig. 4.2 A). Place your right hand on your waist. Bend into the right leg, trying to stack your knee directly over the ankle while keeping the



For any stretch or movement performed where a horse is present, I strongly recommend that he be properly secured, either to a set of cross-ties or with a single safety knot, depending on his training and experience (fig. 4.1 A). I also suggest the rider wear her ASTM-SEI approved safety helmet (with the harness fastened) whenever working around her mount. This includes during the turn in, grooming, and tacking-up phases of her ride (fig. 4.1 B).

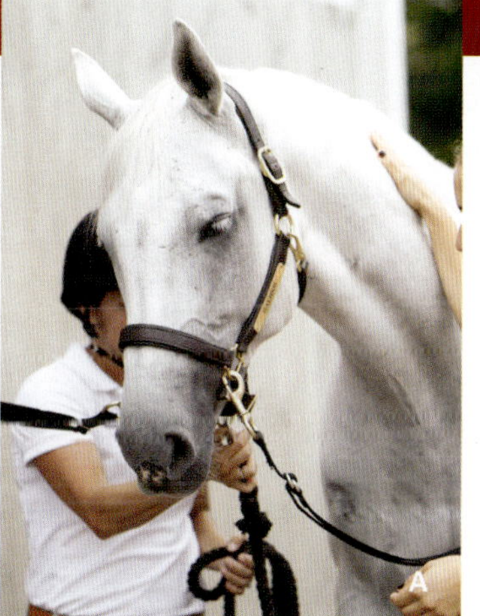

4.1 A | For any of your unmounted warm-up exercises, I recommend your horse be properly secured, either to a set of cross-ties or with a single safety knot.

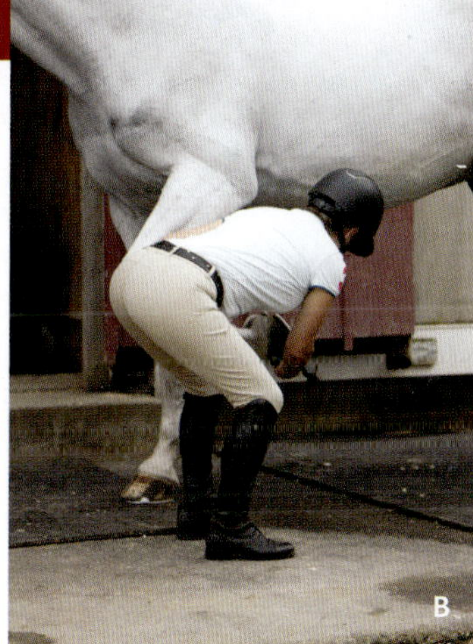

4.1 B | Riders should wear their ASTM-SEI approved helmet whenever working around their mounts, including turn in, grooming, and tacking-up phases of their ride.

4.2 A & B | Loretta has correctly positioned herself three feet away from her tools as she prepares to step forward into the Grooming Box Lunge (A). To pick up your grooming tool, stack your knee directly over the ankle while keeping the pelvis oriented straight ahead. You should feel the stretch on the front of the opposite hip (B).

# "Good Stretch"

When it comes to stretching, how much is "enough"? Is this a case of "No pain, no gain"? What if I do a stretch and I don't really feel...anything?

Any or all of these questions may run through a rider's mind as she goes through a stretching routine—and there are no hard and fast answers. The truth is that some stretches will be easier than others, and how the same stretch feels on one side of the body versus the other may be completely different. When an athlete commits to completing her stretching routine on a regular basis, stretches that once were difficult may gradually become easier. On the other hand, riders with old injuries that have left scar tissue or other physical impair-

ments may never regain the same range of motion they once had—but even so, stretching can still be beneficial. And, of course, in cases of significant previous injury or other restrictions, always consult your medical team regarding how best to proceed for your body.

Regardless of whether you consider yourself to be flexible or not, when it comes to stretching, you are always looking for what I call "Good Stretch." This is the place where the athlete feels the effort of the stretch; sometimes there is a positive feeling of release, but it also may not be wholly comfortable. It is never a place of sharp, intense, dull, or unrelenting pain. Pain is the body's way of telling an athlete she has gone too far.

The rider should begin each stretch slowly, bringing awareness to the sensations in her muscles, ligaments, and tendons, moving until pelvis oriented straight ahead. The left leg is extended behind the hip, with the toe on the ground and the heel up. Reach with the left arm to grab the hoof pick. You should feel the stretch on the front of your left hip, with engagement in your right quadriceps.

After you have picked the horse's feet, reverse the position of each limb to feel the stretch on the opposite side of the body as you return the hoof pick to your box (fig. 4.2 B). Continue the process, alternating sides to retrieve and return each tool, until you have completed the grooming sequence.

## Grooming Stretch #2: Curry Comb Toe Raises

As the name of this movement implies, you will do the Curry Comb Toe Raises while currying your horse's body. This movement is a good strength-builder and balance

*Scan to View Video*

she begins to feel the effort of the stretch. This is "Good Stretch." Depending on the stretch being performed, this is the place to take a few deep breaths in and out, relaxing those muscles that do not need to be engaged to hold the stretch, and allowing the muscle(s) being stretched to find some ease. Release the stretch the same way you came into it—slowly and deliberately.

Even if stretches are being held for a count, try to maintain a smooth and consistent degree of effort. Try not to "pulse" or bounce in the stretch. When riders do this, it becomes easy to accidentally overextend soft tissue through the energy of movement.

If a particular stretch feels quite easy, first review the description of the biomechanics required and rewatch the accompanying video to ensure you are performing it correctly. It may be helpful to perform the stretch in front of a mirror or have a friend video you on her phone to review your body position. Once you have confirmed that the stretch is being practiced with correct alignment, if you are still feeling minimal effect, this is a good moment to consider one of the Upward Modifiers. Depending on the stretch, this can mean adding wrist or ankle weights, moving the grooming box farther away, or widening or deepening a stance.

Finally, it is important to remember that everyone is unique, and not every stretch will work for everybody. If a stretch consistently causes discomfort or pain, or simply does not create the sensation of "good stretch," no matter how it is modified, do not include it in your Equicize routine. Listening to her body, and learning what her body needs, is perhaps one of the most important actions the Everyday Rider can take to ensure success.

4.3 | **The Curry Comb Toe Raise is a good strength builder and balance challenge that is performed while you curry your horse. As you start to curry, slowly begin to rise up onto the balls of both feet. Hold for a count of three, then slowly lower down. Repeat as you work your way around your horse to curry his entire body. Loretta lightly rests one hand on her horse's shoulder to stabilize her balance.**

challenge that is often harder to do than it sounds.

As you start to curry your horse, slowly begin to rise up onto the balls of both feet (fig. 4.3). As you lift up, feel your calves and quadriceps engage. Consciously engage your abdominal muscles by drawing your belly button toward your spine; this will help with your balance. Hold for a count of three, then slowly lower back down. Continue this pattern as you move around your horse's body. Remember to keep breathing!

If you lose your balance, the good news is your horse is there to catch you. But because you will be moving the curry, it will be difficult to cheat by leaning on the horse instead of engaging your legs and abdominals.

## Grooming Stretch #3: Quadriceps Stretch

Once you have finished currying and are moving onto the hard brush, it is time to do the Quadriceps Stretch. Stretch the left leg while brushing the left side of the horse, and stretch the right leg while brushing the right.

This description will match the movements and limb positions for the left side. Simply reverse for side two.

# Check-Out Line Calf Crunches

*Scan to View Video*

Think about your daily routine, and ask yourself how many (minutes, hours) of your life you have spent standing in line. If you are like most of us, I am sure the answer is too large a number to count.

Close your eyes and imagine yourself waiting in line. Maybe it is at the grocery store, or the local coffee shop (fig. 4.4). Perhaps you are at the bank, or even pumping gas. How do you hold your body in these situations? Are you standing tall, with a supportive, lightly engaged core, weight centered equally over both legs? Or, more likely, are you slouched, slumped over a cart, resting one leg, or cocking a hip?

These kinds of habitual asymmetries can become all-too-comfortable and familiar poses for our bodies, and we practice them—constantly and unconsciously—doing everyday activities. Unfortunately, these habits do not disappear when we get on our horse, and they contribute to many of the symmetry and coordination challenges riders experience.

The next time you find yourself yet again waiting in line, try this: find your centered athletic stance, take a deep breath in through your nose, exhale softly out through your mouth, and on your next inhale, slowly rise up onto the balls of your feet, just as if you were doing a Curry Comb Toe Raise. The only difference here is that you can use your car, cart, or counter for stability instead of your horse. If there are no available surfaces to aid your balance, perhaps do not lift as high onto your toes at first. Hold for a count of three, then slowly lower to flat feet, re-center, and repeat.

At first, you may feel self-conscious, but in reality, most everyone else waiting in line will be too focused on their own to-do list, their phone, or finding their wallet to pay much attention to you. Even if you don't complete a Calf Crunch every time you stand in line, simply learning to notice your habitual postures and working to find a more centered and even stance will help improve your overall fitness and symmetry.

**4.4** | The next time you find yourself waiting in line at the grocery store, coffee shop, or feed store, try the Check-Out Line Calf Crunches. Find your centered athletic stance and slowly rise up onto the balls of your feet. Hold for a count of three, then slowly lower to flat feet, re-center and repeat.

4.5 A | While using your hard brush during your grooming routine, transfer your weight onto the right leg. Bend the left knee and reach toward the left ankle with your left hand. Hold the stretch while you flick your hard brush. Stephanie has lightened the intensity of the Quadriceps Stretch by keeping her bent knee both slightly more open and a bit forward of her standing leg.

4.5 B | After completing the Quadriceps Stretch on her left leg, Stephanie transfers her weight onto the left leg. She bends the right knee and reaches toward the right ankle with her right hand.  She holds the stretch while she uses the hard brush.

*Scan to View Video*

Start by rooting down onto the sole of your right boot. Feel all four corners of the foot on the ground and begin transferring your weight onto the right leg. Bend the left knee and reach toward the left ankle with your left hand, trying to make contact (figs. 4.5 A & B). If you can't reach the ankle, grab the shin or any other place on the limb you can connect to. Once you have made contact, pause and find your balance, then use the opposite arm to flick the hard brush. Feel the stretch from the left hip through the front of your thigh (quadriceps) down to your knee.

The goal is to eventually keep the bent knee pointing straight toward the ground. But at first, it may be enough to simply bend the knee, find your balance on the opposite leg, and brush your horse!

If the initial stretch is too much, back off on the intensity by bringing your bent

# Fuel-Station Quad Press

After you have mastered the Quadriceps Stretch during your daily grooming routine, here is a fun variation to practice while pumping gas, working at your stand-up desk, or even waiting for water to boil on the stove!

With your right hand managing the pump (or keyboard or stirring spoon), root down through the sole of your right foot and transfer your weight onto the right leg. Continue to set up for the Quadriceps Stretch, applying whatever modifiers your body requires to be successful. Find your personal edge in this stretch, applying enough pressure to the lower half of your bent left leg so you experience good stretch (fig. 4.6).

While maintaining your sensation of Good Stretch, slowly bend into the right knee. Keep your upper body posture tall, with shoulders stacked in alignment over your hips. Lower your weight down onto the standing leg until you feel the effort of engagement in your right quadriceps. Hold for a count of three, then straighten. Repeat three times, then switch legs.

The Fuel-Station Quad Press combines a stretch with a strengthening movement. As you repeat this exercise, you will likely find that you can add both more stretch into the bent leg and more depth in the bend of the standing leg. As with any Equicize exercise, listen to your body and seek to find your personal edge on that day.

*Scan to View Video*

**4.6 | Tami demonstrates the Fuel-Station Quad Press by grabbing her left ankle with her left hand and holding for a quad stretch. This is a good everyday stretch to do while pumping gas or even waiting for water to boil on the stove.**

knee slightly forward of the standing leg. On the other hand, you can increase the intensity by gently pulling the ankle back and upward. Be sure to listen to your body—it is easy to overstretch.

## Grooming Stretch #4: Lead Rope Shoulder Stretch and Squat

*Scan to View Video*

This stretch will combine arm movements with a leg squat, and is an excellent release if you hold tension in your upper back. It also helps to release the muscles around the rotator cuff in your shoulder so if you have any issues or limitations in this joint, consider the downward modifier or even skipping this stretch altogether.

Place your feet about hip-width apart and bend your knees softly, stacking shoulders over hips (you may recognize this position as athletic stance). Hold your horse's

lead rope in front of you with both hands, keeping tension on the rope between them so that it is held straight, with no slack (figs. 4.7 A–C). While maintaining this tension, lift both arms up over your head, keeping the elbows straight. Start by holding your arms in "neutral"—that is, straight overhead and with your upper arms even with your ears. Slowly and smoothly stretch your arms back behind you, until you feel a gentle stretch in the pectoral muscles of your upper chest and around your shoulders. At the same time, engage your quadriceps and lower yourself down into a squat. Hold for a count of three, then release the arms to neutral, and straighten your legs. Repeat this sequence 10 times.

This movement's combination of stretch and strength makes it a challenging exercise. If coordinating the shoulder stretch with the squat is too much, start with just the arm movements until you become more comfortable performing them. If

4.7 A–C | As Marybeth prepares to execute the Lead Rope Shoulder Stretch and Squat, she holds her lead rope out in front of her, hands slightly wider than shoulder-width, then raises her arms above her head (A). Marybeth lowers into a squat as she begins to draw her arms back (B). Keeping her arms drawn back, she holds the squat for a count of three before releasing the arms to neutral and returning to athletic stance (C).

4.8 A | For athletes who have had rotator cuff surgery or other injuries, Megan demonstrates the modifier for the Lead Rope Shoulder Stretch. Instead of drawing the rope behind the head for the squat, bring the arms forward so the rope can enter your line of sight.

4.8 B The Lead Rope Shoulder Stretch modifier with the arms in front of the body will still allow for a gentle stretch of the shoulder muscles and upper back.

10 repetitions are too many, begin with seven, or five, or three—whatever number causes you to feel the effort of the exercise without going over your personal edge.

For athletes who have had rotator cuff surgery (like myself), you can modify the arm movement as follows. Hold the lead rope as described above and bring your arms to neutral overhead. Instead of drawing the rope backward, bring the arms forward until they are at about 45 degrees—far enough forward that the rope will enter your line of sight (figs. 4.8 A & B). This movement will still allow for a gentle stretch of the shoulder muscles and upper back but puts less strain on those structures supporting the front of the joint.

# Grooming Stretch #5: Soft Brush Squats

Now that your quadriceps and gluteals are feeling warmed up from the Lead Rope Shoulder Stretch and Squat, it is time to give these important muscles a little more attention.

Take two soft brushes, one in each hand, and stand in athletic stance. Lift your arms straight out in front of you until they are even with your shoulders. Engage your quadriceps and core by drawing your belly button toward your spine and squat down, trying to keep your chest open and spine long and tall (figs. 4.9 A & B). At the base of your squat, open both arms to make a "T," keeping them level with your shoulders. Return to standing and bring your arms back in front of you. Repeat 10 times.

4.9 A | Megan demonstrates the Soft Brush Squats by putting a soft brush in each hand and holding them out in front of her body at shoulder-height.

4.9 B | Once Megan has her soft brushes at shoulder-height, she squats down and opens both arms to make a "T." Then she returns to standing and brings her arms back in front of her.

**4.10 A** | If going into a full squat is too much, a good modifier is to use a tack box or hay bale to support your movement. Loretta stands with her backside to the tack box.

**4.10 B** | For the modifier, Loretta stands with her backside to the tack box, then lowers down so her seat bones balance right on the edge of the trunk.

For maximum effect, make each step of the Soft Brush Squat clear and deliberate. It might help to do it in a four-count—arms out straight, squat, arms forward, return to standing. Even though you will quickly realize how tiring it is to hold your arms out straight, this isn't really an arm exercise; it is more about finding your balance and strengthening your legs and core.

If going into a full squat is a bit too much right now, a good modifier is to use a tack box or hay bale to support your movement. Standing with your backside to the tack box, position your hips so that when you go into your squat, you can touch your seat bones to the edge of the trunk (figs. 4.10 A & B). Don't fully put your weight down—you won't be there long!

For greater challenge, athletes have two options—choose one or both! The first

**4.11 A & B** | For a greater challenge for their squats, riders can still hold the brushes but go into a deep squat without the balance of a tack trunk or hay bale. Loretta keeps her feet about shoulder-width apart (A), and keeping her heels flat, closes down until her thigh bone is parallel to the ground (B).

Upward Modifier is to bring the arms straight up overhead instead of out to the sides during the squat phase, being sure to keep the elbow straight. The second Upward Modifier is to deepen the squat, keeping your heels flat and closing down until your femur (thigh bone) is parallel to the ground (figs. 4.11 A & B). This option might be the perfect choice if you regularly do squats during your gym routine and, therefore, have had the opportunity to already develop the strength and balance required for this movement.

## Grooming Stretch #6: Achilles Stretch

The Achilles Stretch is an excellent way to prepare the muscles, tendons, and ligaments of your lower leg for the flexion required to keep your heels lower than your

toes. Many riders tell me they struggle with this essential skill due to stiffness in their ankle joint. If there is no history of injury, oftentimes this "stiffness" is more accurately described as a lack of suppleness in the soft tissues supporting the joint—and that is a condition that systematic stretching is designed to improve.

Transfer your weight onto your right foot and place the ball of your left foot on the edge of your tack box or a hay bale, keeping the pressure evenly distributed across the foot. Your toes should face the ceiling and your heels lower toward the ground. While keeping your shoulders stacked over your hips, gently move into your bent left knee, increasing the pressure on the ball of your left foot (fig. 4.12). When you reach your Good Stretch (the effort is felt in the calves, the Achilles tendon, and depending on how deeply you stretch, the hip flexors on your supporting leg), hold for a count of 10, being sure to keep your inhales and exhales steady. Gently release, and change sides.

Your choice of a tack box or hay bale for this exercise may be logistical (that is, you have access to one item but not the other), but it can also be a form of modifier. Using a tack box similar to the ones in the video will increase the intensity of the stretch because the rider will be lifting her leg higher; using a hay bale or footlocker style tack box will decrease the intensity because the stretch will not be as deep. Depending on your level of flexibility, select the option that challenges your body, and understand that you will still receive a positive benefit, no matter which option you choose.

To add even greater challenge, hold a soft brush in each hand and extend your arms into a "T" shape as you move into your bent knee. Be

4.12 | **Marybeth keeps her shoulders stacked over her hips and moves her weight onto her bent knee, increases the pressure on the ball of her foot, and holds it for a count of 10. The Achilles Stretch is an excellent way to prepare the muscles, tendons, and ligaments of the lower leg for the flexion required to keep the heels down.**

4.13 A | Stephanie demonstrates the upward modifier by holding a soft brush in each hand at shoulder-height.

4.13 B | When Stephanie steps up onto the tack trunk with a soft brush in each hand and lunges forward, it makes this into both a stretch and a balance challenge.

sure to keep the arms level with the shoulders. Adding the arm position makes this into both a stretch and a balance challenge (figs. 4.13 A & B).

## Grooming Stretch #7: Whole Body Stretch

The Whole Body Stretch is the perfect finale to your unmounted warm-up, as it combines elements from several previous stretches and adds mobility.

To get started, set up similarly to the Achilles Stretch: transfer your weight onto your right leg and place the ball of your left foot on the edge of a tack box or hay bale. Bend softly at the waist and extend your left arm down your bent left leg until you are resting your upper arm on the inside of your knee; your left elbow will be just below the knee, and your hand will rest on the inside of the ankle. Turn your palm out. Bring

your right palm to touch your left—you will now be leaning forward slightly, with neck soft and eyes looking down.

For the duration of this stretch, your legs and left arm will remain "as is." But your right arm is going to smoothly lift up toward the sky as you simultaneously rotate your waist away from your bent leg. Try to extend all the way through your fingertips, with your gaze to follow if that feels comfortable (figs. 4.14 A & B). Hold this twist in the waist and extended arm for a breath, then exhale and close, returning your torso to center and your right palm to meet left. Repeat 10 times in as steady a rhythm as possible, then switch sides.

The Whole Body Stretch opens and expands the chest, and is a great antidote to the slumped forward shoulders that come from sitting in front of a computer all day. But it also improves the mobility of the spine, hip, and ankle joints, and challenges balance. After all, this is exactly what you are trying to do while mounted—maintain your balance while also staying supple and fluid on the horse.

4.14 A & B | Megan demonstrates the Whole Body Stretch, the perfect finale to your unmounted warm up. Place the ball of your foot on the edge of a tack box and extend your arm down your bent leg until you are resting your upper arm on the inside of your knee (A). Once you are resting your upper arm on the inside of your knee, the right arm is going to smoothly lift up toward the sky as you rotate your waist away from your bent leg (B).

# A NOTE ON ASYMMETRY

No being—human or equine—has a perfectly symmetrical body. Whether due to genetics, conformation, injury, or fitness routine (or a combination thereof), there will always be a difference in flexibility and  strength between one limb and its partner on the other side, in the alignment of the body, or in a pair of muscles. A thoughtful exercise system or training program helps to make an athlete aware of these asymmetries within her own body and helps her to overcome them.

Asymmetries don't simply disappear when a rider gets on her horse. Instead, a rider's asymmetries will intersect with those of her mount, sometimes leading to great frustration for all involved. Becoming aware of how each of our own bodies is unique in its physical strengths and limitations is the first step toward resolving those limitations in the future. When a thoughtful rider encounters training challenges or resistance in her mount, one of the first areas she will check is to see if her own asymmetries are playing a role in the communication breakdown.

As you work through these unmounted warm-up exercises, begin to notice if one side feels easier or more comfortable than the other, or if you are able to go deeper into the exercise with one limb or the other. Record these observations in your journal.

Over time, experiment with different modifications or numbers of repetitions to see if you can help your "more difficult" side to catch up. Though there are different schools of thought on this subject, I find that rather than going harder or deeper on the "easy" side (which can actually exacerbate the asymmetry), athletes benefit more from doing a few extra "lighter" repetitions on the "difficult" side. For example, if you are doing the Achilles Stretch and realize that you feel less effort or stretch when the left ankle is flexed rather than the right (meaning the left side is the "easy" side and the right side is the "difficult" one), perhaps try starting with the right side, switching to the left, then doing an extra stretch on the right instead of pressing deeper into the left stretch.

# Dr. Hartman's Symmetry Identification and Mobility Correctives

In my travels around the country teaching clinics, I have had the opportunity to meet many like-minded professionals, and I always appreciate these occasions to exchange ideas. Recently, I was able to collaborate with my colleague Dr. Alison Hartman of Pro-Activity's EQFit, who is both a physical therapist and an avid equestrian. Ali has helped me to compile a series of Mobility Correctives, exercises designed to help equestrian athletes become more familiar with their own asymmetries—and I am now sharing that list with you here.

The following series of unmounted exercises can help a rider to both diagnose and correct symmetry issues between sides. We've chosen these specific exercises because they address common areas of asymmetry in riders; as you work through them, you may find that one exercise highlights

*Scan to View Video*

great asymmetry, while another shows that you are fairly equal on both sides. By repeating those exercises that highlight asymmetry, a rider can work toward equalizing her suppleness between both sides of her body. Please note that this set of exercises focuses on mobility corrections; to improve strength or motor control on the weaker side, different exercises may be indicated.

To get started, take some time and work through each of these exercises. Pay special attention to the differences in reach, ease, or comfort between the right and left sides of your body. Sometimes the difference is subtle—but it is still an asymmetry that can be improved through the use of these mobility corrections.

## Mobility Corrective #1: Standing Figure 4 Stretch

The Standing Figure 4 Stretch highlights the mobility of a rider's hips and the soft tissues of her lower back. To begin, transfer your weight onto the sole of your right foot then cross the shin of your left leg across your right thigh; your legs will look like the number "4." (You can use a wall, fence, or tack box to help with your balance throughout this exercise.) Keep your back flat and hinge the hips back, until the stretch is felt in either the front or back of the right hip (fig. 4.15). Go deeper by applying gentle pressure to the right knee and thigh with the right hand. Hold for a count of 10, then release. Reverse the limbs and repeat on the opposite side.

Be sure when doing this stretch that the pelvis stays level—it is easy to collapse it to one side. Pay special attention to any sensation of stiffness, and notice how far you can drop your knee down on one side versus the other. These are both clues to identifying your stiffer side.

To use this exercise as a mobility corrective, repeat this stretch two or three times per side, with a break and reset in between sets.

## Mobility Corrective #2: Anterior Chain Stretch and Sidebend

The Anterior Chain Stretch will address a myriad of interconnected muscles that run largely along the front of the rider's body, like the hip flexors. But adding the Sidebend will also bring attention to some of the rider's back muscles, including the latissimus dorsi and lateral trunk and lower back muscles such as the quadratus lumborum. She may also feel a stretch in the calf of the back leg.

From a standing position, take a large step back with your right leg, making sure the toes

4.15 | Dr. Ali Hartman, both a physical therapist and an avid equestrian, demonstrates a series of unmounted exercises to help riders with asymmetries. The Standing Figure 4 Stretch helps stretch the rider's hips and lower back. Cross the shin of your right leg across your left thigh and hold for a count of 10.

of both feet stay pointed straight forward, legs roughly hip-width apart. Slowly sink the back heel toward the ground and allow the left leg to bend softly (fig. 4.16 A). Depending on your flexibility, the right heel may either touch the ground or remain elevated. Find your own edge, but keep those toes pointed forward.

4.16 A | Dr. Hartman begins the Anterior Chain Stretch and Sidebend mobility corrective by taking a large step back with her right leg and sinking the back heel toward the ground.

4.16 B │ **Shift your weight forward into the bent front leg and reach both arms overhead while continuing to support your spine.**

4.16 C │ **With both arms overhead, Dr. Hartman adds a very gentle side stretch. Hold for a count of five, release, and repeat on the opposite side.**

Check here that you are not arching the back, pressing the rib cage forward, or jutting your chin and stiffening the neck. Keep your rib cage tucked down and back flat by gently engaging your core, and draw your chin underneath your forehead, releasing the muscles of the neck. Shift your weight forward into the bent front leg while simultaneously thinking about opening the front of your back hip. Continue to shift forward until you feel a good stretch, take a few breaths, then see if you can lower your heel a tiny bit more on an exhale (fig. 4.16 B).

Now, reach both arms overhead while continuing to support your spine with an engaged core. The goal here is not to arch the back but rather to stretch up through the side of the body to intensify the stretch. Only once you have found this length in the side of the body, and only if it is comfortable, should you add a very gentle side stretch, taking both arms toward the side of the bent right leg while maintaining your body position from the hips down. Hold for a count of five, release, and repeat on the opposite side.

As you do the Anterior Chain Stretch and Sidebend, take note of how far you can sink down right versus left, as well as whether it is easier to keep the toes straight in one direction versus the other. As you gain mobility, it will become possible to deepen the stretch both by going farther forward into the bent leg and bringing the heel closer to the ground.

## Mobility Stretch #3: Seated Twist

The Seated Twist is an excellent exercise to improve the mobility of the rider's spine, pectorals, and hips. This variation is designed to be barn-friendly and can be practiced using a tack trunk, mounting block, or other similar sturdy and level surface.

Sit on the tack trunk and position your feet slightly wider than hip-width apart, with your toes even and slightly pointed out. Lean gently forward and rest your elbows on your thighs.

Stay here, or, depending on how flexible you are, reach your arms all the way down the insides of your legs to touch your ankles or even the tops of your feet. Find your edge—any variation is correct if it brings you to good stretch.

Slowly extend your left arm toward the sky, rotating your torso toward the left and opening your chest (fig. 4.17 A). If it is comfortable, your gaze can follow the tips of your fingers on your extended arm. Feel the chest-opening effect of this movement,

**4.17 A & B** | The Seated Twist improves the mobility of the rider's spine, pectorals, and hips. Find a sturdy and level surface such as a tack trunk or mounting block and lean forward and rest your elbows on your thighs. Reach down and touch your ankles, or your shins if you can't get that far, and extend your left arm toward the sky, rotating your torso (A). Switch sides and stretch your opposite side (B). When you twist on each side, notice whether you can rotate as freely or as far in both directions.

and the gentle stretch in your pectoral (chest) muscles. Take a breath in and out with your arm in extension, then return to your original position. Switch sides (fig. 4.17 B).

When you do the Seated Twist, notice whether you can rotate as freely or as far in both directions. Over time, see if you can work through the resting-arm position options (resting on elbows, then reaching to ankles, then to tops of feet) as your mobility improves.

4.18 A | **The Posterior Chain Lengthener addresses the mobility in many of the muscle groups that oppose those that are activated in the Anterior Chain Stretch. Stand in your athletic stance and step the left leg forward. Straighten the left knee while flexing the ankle and lifting the toe.**

## Mobility Stretch #4: Posterior Chain Lengthener

The Posterior Chain Lengthener addresses the mobility in many of the muscle groups that oppose those that are activated in the Anterior Chain Stretch. With the Posterior Chain Lengthener, we will be stretching the hamstrings, gluteal muscles, and calves. These muscles help the rider to keep her legs long and underneath her hips while mounted; they also help her to maintain the toe-up/heel-down position required in most riding disciplines.

Start by finding your athletic stance, weight centered over both feet and knees softly bent. Transfer your weight onto the right foot, keeping the soft knee bend, and step the left leg forward (fig. 4.18 A). Straighten the left knee while flexing the ankle and lifting the toe. You will now be resting the heel of your left extended leg on the ground (fig. 4.18 B). Hinge at the hips, keeping a neutral spine and engaged core, until a good stretch is felt down the back of the left leg or calf. Be careful to avoid simply bending at the waist—your back needs to be supported with the core.

While holding this position, alternate pointing then flexing the left foot for 10 repetitions (fig. 4.18 C). Return to standing and repeat on the opposite side.

The muscles of the posterior chain are often tighter or less supple than their anterior counterparts, and many riders will notice a sometimes significant difference here between the right and left legs. Pay special attention to how far you can hinge before you feel the sensation of stretch on your left side versus the right.

## Mobility Stretch #5: Ankle Mobilizer

The Ankle Mobilizer helps to address restricted movement in the ankle joint and soft tissue of the calf; indirectly, it also can improve mobility in the knee and hip, though these joints are not the primary focus.

This exercise will require the rider to wear a short boot. When the boot has laces or a zipper, loosen the fastening to maximize the effect of this stretch.

Find an elevated surface like a hay bale, tack box, or mounting block. Ideally, position this tool

4.18 B & C | Hinge at the hips, keeping a neutral spine and engaged core until a stretch is felt down the back of the calf (B). While holding this position, alternate pointing and then flexing the left foot for 10 repetitions (C).

4.19 A | The Ankle Mobilizer helps to address restricted movement in the ankle joint and soft tissue of the calf. If you are wearing tall boots, you'll need to unzip the boot to maximize the effect and if you are wearing short boots, loosen the laces. Step up with one leg onto a hay bale, tack trunk, or mounting block, keeping your heel down.

**4.19 B & C** | Bringing the knee as far forward as you can over your foot without lifting your heel, take the knee forward and out until it is in line with the pinky toe of the foot (B). Finish by taking the knee forward and in until it is line with the big toe of the foot (C). Take note if one of the variations reveals greater stiffness in your ankle joint than the others.

so that you can reach a wall or fence in front of you for stability while doing the stretch.

Place your entire left foot flat on the elevated surface, keeping your heel down (fig. 4.19 A). Bring the left knee as far forward as you can over your foot without lifting your heel, stopping when you feel a stretch on the front or back of the ankle. Hold here for a beat, then return to neutral. Now, take the left knee forward then gently press it out, keeping the heel down, until it is in line with the pinky toe of your left foot (fig. 4.19 B). Hold here, then return to neutral. Finally, take the left knee forward and in, toward your big toe, again keeping the heel flat on the surface (fig. 4.19 C). Return to neutral. Repeat three to five times, then switch sides.

Each of these three positions addresses a different facet of ankle mobility. Notice how far forward you can bring your knee before the heel wants to lift, or if one of these variations reveals greater stiffness in your ankle joint than the others.

# PART IV

# Mounted Equicize Routine

# Mounted Equicize
# Warm-Up

In Part III, I introduced you to the unmounted Equicize warm-up. These exercises help to stretch muscles, ligaments, and tendons critical for effective riding, while also building strength and improving balance in the rider. The mounted Equicize warm-up continues to work on these qualities but also begins to increase the rider's cardiovascular effort. The exercises in the mounted Equicize warm-up sequence are designed to coordinate the efforts of several muscle groups at once; after performing them, the rider should feel as though every major athletic system in her body has become activated.

In my first book, *The Athletic Equestrian,* I devote an entire chapter to a series of mounted stretches and other warm-up exercises for riders to use in their daily practice. These are usually performed while the horse is doing his own "walking warm-up," and take about 10 minutes to complete (fig. 5.1). These exercises can be used in conjunction with the mounted Equicize warm-up I am about to describe, or riders can choose to save this series for non-Equicize days. It really comes down to your personal level of fitness, your long-term goals, and what you are hoping to achieve with your individual workout!

Before beginning your mounted Equicize warm-up, it is essential that the horse is allowed at least five minutes of walking on a loose rein as well as five minutes total of posting trot, including work in both directions. As mentioned earlier, Equicize will cause the rider to move in unusual ways on the horse's back and will challenge the rider's balance and coordination. It isn't fair to ask the horse to carry the rider through these exercises without first giving him the opportunity to become physically ready to compensate for his passenger's movements and asymmetry. Further, once you move

5.1 | Time permitting, you can do the unmounted warm-up exercises, the mounted warm-up exercises, then proceed into your mounted Equicize warm-up. Simone warms up her hip flexors by doing her mounted warm-up sequence.

into the warm-up exercises themselves, be sure to change directions frequently so your horse is not bearing more of the effort on one pair of legs than the other.

When riders are trying the mounted Equicize warm-up sequence for the first time, I recommend practicing each exercise at the halt, then the walk, before attempting it in trot. Although several of the exercises utilize the dynamic energy of the trot's two-beat rhythm and can actually be more challenging to perform at the halt or in the walk, it is often easier to double-check alignment, balance, and form at these slower speeds. Some riders need to continue to practice at the halt or in the walk for several sessions, until their confidence, balance, and strength improve. Returning to one of these slower paces is always an option when a rider finds a particular exercise to be challenging—even if it is one she has been successful with in the past. Remember, every day is different, and your body will not respond the same way to each workout!

There are four exercises to complete during the mounted Equicize warm-up sequence: Mounted Torso Twists, Hip-Forward Pencil Stands, Sit-Ones, and Stand-Ones.



"Outside" and "inside" are two words commonly used by riding instructors. For clarity, when they are used in this book, "outside" indicates the side of the arena along the wall, fence, or edge, while "inside" refers to the middle, center, or interior of the riding space.

## Mounted Warm-Up #1: Mounted Torso Twist

*Scan to View Video*

The Mounted Torso Twist uses the dynamic movement of the horse to help unlock the muscles of the shoulder and back, and to increase the suppleness of the spine and hips. When practiced at the walk, the exercise mainly works to increase suppleness in the soft tissues supporting the bones and joints in the rider's hips and back. At the trot, the Mounted Torso Twist also becomes a balance and coordination challenge, adding increased core engagement to the benefits received in the walk.

The Mounted Torso Twist is all about the upper body. It is important that the rider's pelvis stays square to the front; the rider's left hip bone should point toward the horse's left ear, and the right hip bone toward his right ear. Slide your legs slightly forward into Power Leg (see p. 32), so they stay steady and stable when you begin to twist your torso.

Try the Mounted Torso Twist first at the halt or in the walk, facing or tracking left.

5.2 A | Marianne demonstrates the Mounted Torso Twist by keeping her hips square to the front and twisting her upper torso to the outside of the arena. The Torso Twist helps the rider to unlock her spine, rib cage, and shoulder and back muscles.

Begin by checking your overall alignment. Are your shoulders stacked over your hips? Do you feel your right and your left seat bones equally? Slide into Power Leg. Notice if this affects your alignment; if it does, come back to center before going farther.

Now, begin to rotate your waist toward the outside of the arena, without losing the forward alignment of the hips or lifting the inside seat bone off the saddle. Rotate the waist and shoulders as far as you can without losing the alignment in the hips, with the goal of facing your open shoulders at the outside wall. Your head and gaze will remain facing forward, over your left shoulder—remember, you still need to steer (figs. 5.2 A & B)! If you are trying this at the halt, hold for a count of 10, focusing on

**5.2 B | Morgan also demonstrates the Mounted Torso Twist. I have my riders perform the Torso Twist to the outside only because the fence or wall helps to support the direction of travel. After completing it on the right rein, switch to the left rein in order to twist both sides of the body.**

keeping both your in and out breath steady and strong. If you are trying this at the walk, hold the Mounted Torso Twist as you ride down the long side of the arena, and return to center at the short end. Repeat on the next long side.

A few important notes—first, it is important the rider does not accidentally pull back on her outside rein when her outside shoulder rotates out. I have my riders consciously touch their knuckles together in front of them before beginning the twist, and maintain this hand position throughout. Secondly, I only have riders perform the Mounted Torso Twist to the outside, because the fence or wall of the arena helps support the horse's direction of travel. Horses tend to follow our weight in the saddle, and despite their best effort, most riders find their weight shifting slightly in the direction of their twist. Especially if you are riding with a group, it is important for safety that the horses stay on the rail. When riders twist to the inside, inevitably, their mount moves in that direction.

After you have completed the Mounted Torso Twist to the right (while the horse is tracking left), change direction, and reverse the movements listed above to complete the Twist to the left.

Only after the rider is fairly comfortable with both the position and muscle engagement required to perform the Mounted Torso Twist at the walk should she attempt it at the posting trot. For the well-being of the horse, this exercise should never be practiced at the sitting trot—even in a Western saddle.

## Mounted Warm-Up #2: Hip-Forward Pencil Stand

This exercise is a challenging standing balance that will also help riders develop strength in their legs, gluteal muscles, and abdominal core. The goal is to stand straight up in the saddle, keeping the ankle flexed and knee soft, while bringing the hips forward until the rider's center is aligned with the pommel. This is absolutely not a position a rider would adopt during a normal ride, but when used for strength- and balance-building, it is perfect form.

*Scan to View Video*

## THE EQUICIZE COUNT

Throughout this book, I use the term "count" in reference to the amount of time a rider should hold a balance challenge, or the number of repetitions of a particular movement or exercise. In Equicize, the "count" is coordinated with the two-beat rhythm of the trot. Count ONE for the upbeat, and TWO for the downbeat; to count a repetition, count ONE, two, TWO, two, THREE, two, and so on, until you reach the correct count total.

This method applies even during balance challenges (like the Hip-Forward Pencil Stand), in which the rider is not actually posting, as well as in exercises like Sit-Ones and Stand-Ones, where she is regularly changing her diagonal. Always count the upbeat as ONE and the downbeat as TWO to maintain a consistent rhythm.

Here's how to do it:

1. Place your lower leg into Power Leg. This is critical to help maintain a base of support and balance when you are at the top of your Stand. Be sure to keep a soft flexion in the ankles and allow the heels to drop lower than the toes.

2. Start to lift your seat out of the saddle, opening your knee angles while engaging your calves and quadriceps. Be mindful to keep the knee soft; once it is open all the way, don't allow it to lock.

3. Continue to rise up, opening the hip angle, until your center (an imaginary point behind your belly button and about an inch in front of your spine) is aligned with the pommel of your saddle. Western riders should come as close as they can to standing over the pommel or center themselves over the swell (fig. 5.3 A).

4. Hold for a count of five, then slowly and with control, lower your seat into the saddle.

No matter what their chosen discipline, I find that most riders do not push their hips far enough forward. Remember, it is called the Hip-Forward Pencil Stand, and it is important to work toward keeping the hip angles open. To help find the correct mechanic, think about tucking the tailbone forward by engaging the core and flattening the lower back. For some riders, it helps to imagine they are imitating the figurehead sculpture on the bow of a tall sailing ship (fig. 5.3 B).

Once a rider has practiced this position at the halt and/or walk, it is time to try it in the trot (fig. 5.4). Initially, hold the Hip-Forward Pencil Stand for a count of five, then post a few beats to reset before trying it again. Do this for an entire circuit of the arena. As you get stronger and more confident, try holding the Hip-Forward Pencil Stand for a slowly increasing count, adding a few more beats at a time. Eventually, you may be able to hold the Hip-Forward Pencil Stand for an entire circuit, with no breaks or loss of balance.

**5.3 A & B** | Tami shows the Hip-Forward Pencil Stand at the halt (A). This position will help riders develop strength in their legs, gluteal muscles, and abdominal core. This is NOT a position a rider should adopt during a normal ride—only use it for strength and balance-building. To help find the correct mechanic in the Hip-Forward Pencil Stand, I ask riders to imagine they are imitating the figurehead sculpture on the bow of a tall sailing ship (B).

5.4 | Once the rider has practiced the Pencil Stand at the halt or walk, I ask her to move into the trot and hold the position for a count of five, post a few beats, then hold for a count of five. Here, Amanda is holding the Pencil Stand for a count of five.

Although it is most important to focus on finding your personal edge when completing these exercises, once riders have built up a base of fitness, it can be a fun group challenge to see who can hold her Hip-Forward Pencil Stand the longest.

## Mounted Warm-Up #3: Sit-Ones

Each of our next two exercises—Sit-Ones and Stand-Ones—play with the rider's ability to control and resist the following movement of her body in the posting trot. A rider who is just learning to post lacks this control, and until she finds it, will simply bounce along in the horse's two-beat rhythm. This is obviously not comfortable for horse or rider, and typically helps motivate a new rider to figure out how to use the thrust of the trot's moment of suspension (the split second when all four of the horse's legs are off the ground during the trot, canter, and gallop) to coordinate her movements.

*Scan to View Video*

Even before this rider learns to recognize her posting diagonals, her instructor likely has cued her to change from the "wrong" diagonal to the "correct" diagonal by sitting for an extra beat. For our purposes, the "correct" diagonal is when the rider rises up in coordination with the forward swing of the horse's outside fore and inside hind; she sits when this diagonal pair of limbs swings back. In competitive English riding, the only correct method of changing from the "wrong" diagonal to the "correct" diagonal is by sitting an extra beat.

Sit-Ones are easiest to do in the trot. Note that I said "easiest," and not "easy"— Sit-Ones are almost guaranteed to help riders work up a sweat! However, it is possible to practice them first at the walk or even the halt—but this will require the rider to fully draw on the strength of her legs to fight gravity and lift her seat out of the saddle. Assuming that our Everyday Rider already is comfortable and familiar with the posting trot, I will proceed to explain how to do the Sit-Ones in that gait.

Start by establishing a positive forward trot, tracking left. Begin posting on the correct diagonal (fig. 5.5). Post for a count of five, then sit one beat and post on the "wrong" diagonal for a count of five. Remember to count each time you are in the "up" beat of your posting trot. Complete one circuit of the arena while repeating this pattern.

5.5 | Sit-Ones play with the rider's ability to control and resist the following movement of her body in the posting trot. Here, Loretta is doing the most difficult modifier by performing her Sit-Ones with no stirrups.

At first, this may be enough to fully challenge your ability to balance, engage the core, and deliberately control your posting rhythm. When it starts to feel easy, progressively increase the challenge by adding extra circuits with a decreasing count. After completing a circuit of "fives," try one circuit of posting for four, then sitting for one. Later, try adding a circuit of "threes" (post for three, sit for one), then "twos" (post for two, sit for one).

I don't recommend performing a circuit of "ones," where the rider would be changing her diagonal every stride. Not only is it incredibly difficult to maintain any sort of steady rhythm, it is also too easy to cause discomfort to the horse's back.

**5.6 A & B** | **Stand-Ones both challenges the rider's balance and encourages her to engage her core. Loretta is performing Stand-Ones with no stirrups, which is the hardest variation (A). Loretta is in the sitting portion of her posting trot after standing a beat to get onto the opposite diagonal (B).**

## Mounted Warm-Up #4: Stand-Ones

Our final mounted Equicize warm-up exercise is called Stand-Ones. Stand-Ones are functionally the opposite of the Sit-Ones, and you will practice them the same way, beginning with a circuit of "fives," then adding "fours," "threes," and "twos." The difference is that instead of sitting for the extra beat to change diagonals, the rider will stand an extra beat. This both challenges the rider's balance and encourages her to engage her core (figs. 5.6 A & B).

*Scan to View Video*

Be mindful while practicing the Stand-Ones to not use the reins for balance. If you feel unstable or as though you might fall back into the tack, grab some mane to regain control of your balance, or return to your posting rhythm for a few beats to reset.

# Leg Builders

Perhaps one of the most important things a rider can do to ensure she feels safe and secure in the saddle is to develop strength and consistency in her leg position. When a rider has a solid lower leg that stays correctly in place under her hip even if the horse trips, spooks, or does something else unexpected, it is probably the closest she can come to wearing a seat belt while in the saddle.

One of the fastest and most effective ways to strengthen and tone the leg muscles that riders need to achieve this security is to practice the two-point position. When I teach novice riders—even if they have no intention of learning to jump—I always include two-point in their early lessons. Two-point is so important to a rider's overall fitness that when I created Equicize, the position became an essential component to the entire system.

The two exercises in this chapter—Two-Point/Chest Press and One-Handed Chest Press—are based off the rider's ability to execute a correctly balanced two-point position. If this is a new position for you, be sure to review "Two-Point Fundamentals for Equicize," back in chapter 3 (p. 27), before proceeding further. But riders will also need to practice another new position to do these exercises—Chest Press. Chest Press is often novel even to jumping riders, and I will break it down in more detail in the sidebar on the next page.

Not only are these two exercises guaranteed to bring a bit of heat to your leg muscles, they will also elevate your heart and respiratory rates. As you begin to practice this sequence, be sure to listen to your body and take short rest breaks as needed. It is more useful to do fewer repetitions correctly than many repetitions in poor balance or incorrect form.

## Leg Builder #1: Two-Point/Chest Press

Once a rider has practiced the transition from two-point to Chest Press at the halt and walk, she is ready to take it into the trot. In this exercise, the rider will coordinate her transitions between these two positions with the horse's stride.

To get started, establish a positive forward posting trot. Choose a marker along your arena (fence posts can work well if you don't have arena letters) and transition to two-point at that marker. Hold your two-point for a count of five, then transition to Chest Press for a count of five. Continue alternating between these two positions on a count of five for two full circuits (figs. 6.1 A & B).

*Scan to View Video*

**6.1 A & B** | **Reina performs the Two-Point/Chest Press by starting off in the two-point position and holding it for a count of five (A). Reina now transitions to her Chest Press position and holds for a count of five (B).**

# Chest Press

The Chest Press is essentially an ultra-deep two-point position, used to help riders home in on their center of balance and to build strength. It is not a position riders would typically use while navigating a course of jumps or out on a foxhunt, and in my experience, even seasoned jumping riders find Chest Press to be a challenge, at least at first.

Because Chest Press is based on the two-point, let's first do a quick check-in on your technique in this position. Starting in the halt or walk:

1. Slide your lower leg into Power Leg.

2. Engage your leg muscles and lift your seat from the saddle.

3. Sink your weight into your heel and ensure your ankle, knee, and hip angles close.

4. Check that your center is over your horse's center, not over the pommel of the saddle.

After making any required adjustments to your position, transition into posting trot for a few strides, then reestablish your two-point position. When the rider adopts the two-point position in the trot, the energy involved in the movement of the horse's limbs and his moment of suspension radiates through the rider's body, challenging both her position and balance. If you find that your upper body tips forward or you collapse onto the horse's neck, it is most likely that your lower leg has slipped back. Return to walk, reset the Power Leg, then try again. If you are falling back into the saddle, check that your lower leg hasn't slid too far forward. This can happen especially when a rider's stirrups are too long, making it difficult to close the shock-absorbing angles of the ankle, knee, and hip. Only after a rider is fairly comfortable with the two-point will she be ready to attempt a Chest Press.

When you feel confident in your two-point, try the Chest Press as follows. Start in a balanced two-point at the halt or walk. From two-point, close down the angle of your hip even farther, pressing your seat back toward the cantle, until your pelvis is almost parallel

**6.2 A** | Tami performs the two-point as her starting position to learn the Chest Press. She makes sure her legs are underneath her seat and placed in the Power Leg, then rises her seat up out of the saddle without straightening her knee angle.

to your thighs (figs. 6.2 A & B). Your back remains flat, and your chest is pressed down toward the horse's neck. Your arms and hands can stay out ahead of you along the horse's crest, as though you are performing a crest release. Until you get stronger, press your hands down onto the crest, or even grab some mane, to increase your stability. Over time, work toward the goal of holding your balance in Chest Press without this modifier. A correct Chest Press almost looks as if the rider is lying upon her horse's neck—but instead, her leg and back muscles are active and engaged, supporting her upper body.

Performing either the two-point or Chest Press at the halt or walk challenges a rider's strength immensely, as there is no energy from the horse to help her stay out of the saddle. However, it is much easier to correct position, alignment, and balance issues at these slower speeds. If a rider is practicing her Chest Press at the trot and gets discombobulated, she should return to either posting trot or the walk to get reset and re-centered.

**6.2 B** | Once Tami is well balanced in the two-point, she folds deeper into her Chest Press, pressing her seat toward the cantle with a flat back. A correct Chest Press almost looks as if the rider is lying upon her horse's neck, but instead, her leg and back muscles are active and engaged.

As a rider becomes fitter and more comfortable executing two circuits of Two-Point/Chest Press on the five count, it is time to add on. As you approach the arena marker after completing two circuits of "fives," keep going, but transition to holding the two-point for a count of four, then Chest Press for a count of four. Repeat this sequence for one full circuit.

Over time, riders will continue to build until they can successively complete:

- Two circuits of fives (hold two-point for a five count, then Chest Press for a five count).

- One circuit of fours (hold two-point for a four count, then Chest Press for a four count).

- One circuit of threes (hold two-point for a three count, then Chest Press for a three count).

- One circuit of twos (hold two-point for a two count, then Chest Press for a two count).

## COUNTING CIRCUITS AND CHOOSING YOUR CHALLENGE

Although we perform most of the mounted warm-up exercises for one circuit each, I prefer to start with two full circuits of Two-Point/Chest Press. This ensures the rider is truly executing the correct leg and body technique in each position, while also beginning to increase her cardiovascular output. Riders quickly become aware which of their muscles are up to the challenge, and which are just "along for the ride."

If at first two circuits of this exercise at the trot are not possible, make it your goal to work up to that duration for maximum benefit. And if practicing Two-Point/Chest Press at the trot is simply too much for your body right now, you will still receive tremendous benefit from performing this exercise at the walk. Use the same five count, and beginning with the two-point, alternate between these two positions for one full circuit. The slower speed and lack of impulsion in the walk will still offer plenty of challenge for riders who choose to use this modifier!

I can assure you that after completing five successive circuits of Two-Point/Chest Press on a decreasing count, your heart and respiratory rates will be up and the sweat will be pouring down!

An important note: I do not recommend doing counts of one. With "ones," the required transition between the two positions is so quick that riders almost universally switch to using their back muscles instead of their legs. This is incorrect biomechanically and defeats the purpose of the exercise. We want the Everyday Rider's legs to do the heavy lifting!

For many riders, working up to completing the full sequence successively—fives, fours, threes, and twos—will be plenty of effort. But if it starts to feel easy, change rein, and work up to repeating the sequence again. Alternatively, riders can add additional circuits to each count. And when even that feels too easy, try it without stirrups. Remember, it is up to you to determine your personal edge.

Throughout this process, pay close attention to your heart rate and breath. As bodies fatigue, some riders hold their breath, while others breathe faster and faster, restricting their chest muscles. It is important to maintain a steady flow of oxygen to help fuel your muscles, so if you notice your breath has become inconsistent, this is a good cue to back off the intensity by returning to the posting trot for a circuit, or even taking a walk break.

*Scan to View Video*

## Leg Builder #2: One-Handed Chest Press

Once riders have become familiar with executing the Chest Press through the Two-Point/Chest Press sequence, One-Handed Chest Press takes the effort up a notch by adding in both a balance challenge and an abdominal workout. As always, try this exercise at the halt or walk first to develop correct form, progressing to the trot only after you are confident in your movements.

*Scan to View Video*

Begin by tracking left. Transfer both reins into the right hand (see sidebar on p. 85 for several of my favorite methods for doing this), then lift your body into a correctly balanced two-point position.

Next, take your free, left arm, open your palm, and place your fingertips behind your neck. If this is not possible, riders can modify by placing their fingers on the front

# Protect Your Back

Two-Point/Chest Press is sure to get your blood moving and to build some heat in those muscles—but which muscles, specifically, should be feeling the effort?

If an Everyday Rider is executing each position correctly, the majority of the effort in Two-Point/Chest Press should be felt in her calves, quadriceps, and hamstrings. As her legs fatigue, a rider might notice the effort coming through in her lower back. Again, this is a good cue to take a quick break to reset.

Occasionally, I have had riders experience pain in their back while doing this exercise. If this happens to you, STOP IMMEDIATELY. Effort is one sensation, pain is another. Pain is your body's way of communicating that you have exceeded its capacity to perform.

Any time a rider tells me that she is feeling the effort of Two-Point/Chest Press in her back, I check a few important details. First, I ensure that her stirrups are short enough to create sufficient bend in the ankle, knee, and hip; if these joints' angles are too open, it will stress the back (fig. 6.3).

Second, I recheck her biomechanics in the two-point. Is her back flat? Is she engaging her legs as she transitions from seat-in-the-saddle to seat-out-of-the-saddle? Is she maintaining her Power Leg?

Finally, I will have her return to the

6.3 | Madison's stirrup length is too long for her two-point work, which can lead to back fatigue and an inability to stay up in the two-point.

Two-Point/Chest Press in the walk, closely observing her biomechanics to ensure that she is executing each position correctly, in balance and alignment with her horse. If you are working on your own, have a friend take a short video on a phone for you to review.

If, despite these checks and adjustments, problems or pain persist, consult a medical professional for advice before attempting this sequence again.

of their left shoulder or upper left chest. Bend laterally at the waist and stretch the left elbow toward the left knee. Hold here for a count of four, then engage your obliques and return your upper body to center for a count of four. Once you have mastered this movement at the slower speeds, try it in the trot. Work up to completing one full circuit of the arena, repeating the same pattern and count of movement as at the walk. Change direction, and do the same thing on the other side (figs. 6.4 A–C).

I will warn you right now—One-Handed Chest Press is hard. At first, it may only be possible to stretch the elbow toward the middle of your thigh. Maybe you can only manage the movement in your body while your horse is standing still or moving at the walk. Meet



The obliques are located just below the skin on the sides of our bodies, along the ribcage. They help to rotate and bend the torso, and provide stability to the upper body.

**6.4 A | One-Handed Chest Press takes the effort up a notch by adding in both a balance challenge and an abdominal workout. Reina transfers her reins and crop into her left hand and takes her right, free hand and places her fingers behind her neck.**

your body wherever it is, and set small goals of increasing intensity and duration as you gain strength and endurance. Even though it is a challenging exercise, I guarantee that these small steps will add up over time.

For safety, I never have riders perform a One-Handed Chest Press toward their outside knee. It is too easy to hit the wall or fence with your head.

**6.4 B & C** | Reina bends laterally at the waist and stretches her right elbow toward her right knee (B). Once Reina touches her elbow to her right knee, she holds it for a count of four and then returns her upper body to center for a count of four (C). Try to work up to alternating counts of four for an entire circuit, gradually adding circuits as your skill and stamina improves.

# Three Ways to Hold Two Reins in One Hand

*Scan to View Video*

In order to execute a One-Handed Chest Press correctly, riders will need to coordinate not only holding both reins in one hand but steering that way as well. Now, for my Western riders, this is an everyday skill, but for English riders who are more accustomed to steering with two hands and whose horses are rarely trained to neck rein, navigating with both reins in one hand is yet another new skill to master.

There are three ways riders can achieve this:

## Option #1: Tie Your Reins in a Knot

For Equicize riders doing these exercises for the first time, the simplest and most efficient way to manage both reins in one hand is to tie them in a knot, then let the knot rest on the horse's crest. Start by getting into your two-point and determine where along the crest you naturally want to hold your reins while in this position. If you are executing the two-point correctly, your hands should move somewhere between one-third and one-half of the way up the horse's neck, maintaining contact with the horse's mouth. This is the place at which to tie the knot (fig. 6.5 A). If instead you tie the knot where you hold your hands in the walk, the reins will be too long when you are in two-point.

6.5 A | Many of the Equicize exercises are performed with one hand on the reins. One way to hold your reins in one hand is to tie them in a knot. Tami has tied her Western reins in a knot, making sure to tie them short enough so that the horse can feel the contact.

Once the reins are knotted, place your steering hand in front of the knot, splitting your fingers between the two reins. If the left hand is holding the reins, use the index and middle finger to control the right rein, and the ring and pinky fingers to control the left. If necessary, slide all your fingers around either rein for greater strength and intensity.

Some rein styles will naturally loosen from the knot as you are riding—this is especially true with rubber reins. When this happens, simply pause, retie the knot, and continue from where you left off.

## Option #2: Bridge Your Reins

Bridging the reins is a popular technique used when a horse is at risk of becoming strong or otherwise pulling down on the rider's hands, particularly when riding out in the open. Because many riders have been taught to bridge the reins for other purposes, sometimes this becomes the easiest option when it comes time to hold both reins in one hand for Equicize (fig. 6.5 B).

If you are not familiar with bridging the reins, or can't figure out how to transition a two-handed bridge to a one-handed version, try this:

Start with one rein in each hand. To create a right bridge (freeing your left hand), reach across the horse's withers with your right hand while still holding the right rein. Now, grab the left rein (releasing your left hand) and lay the left rein on top of the right. Slide your right hand on the reins until you are holding them at the point where the two reins cross, with your four fingers on top and

6.5 B | Another way to hold the reins when using only one hand is to bridge your reins by crossing the reins across each other so they form "one" rein. Tami then slides her index around the one rein, her pinky around the other rein and the remaining middle fingers on the center reins.

thumb on bottom. Slide the right index finger out and wrap it around the left rein; keep your middle and ring fingers in the middle, and then slide your pinky around the bottom (right) rein. The index finger steers to the left, the middle and ring fingers apply the brakes, and the pinky steers to the right.

**6.5 C** | One of the easiest ways to hold the reins in one hand is to use the Correct Connect Aaron Vale Rein. These reins are held differently than regular reins by wrapping two fingers around the top "branch" of the pad and two fingers around the bottom "branch" of the pad. Then Megan simply transfers the left rein into her right hand.

Reverse the rein and finger positions to create a left bridge, which frees the right hand.

## Option #3: Use the Correct Connect Aaron Vale Rein with 3 Padded Hand Grips

I first introduced you to these innovative training reins back in chapter 2 (p. 11), but now I can better explain why they are so useful. These reins are designed with an adjustable buckle, making them adaptable to equines of all sizes, and the padded hand grips are just so easy to place into one hand.

If you are using the Correct Connect Aaron Vale Rein, hold the grips with your ring and pinky fingers below the grip. The rein runs between the ring and middle fingers, and your middle and index fingers and thumb wrap around the grip. To transfer both reins into one hand, simply line up the grips and double up your hold (fig. 6.5 C).

# The Seated Adductor Squeeze

Your adductor muscles are responsible for moving your legs back toward your body's midline and play an important role in helping riders to both stay in the saddle and give effective, coordinated aids. The Seated Adductor Squeeze helps unmounted riders to engage some of the same ligaments, tendons, and muscles they will activate in the half-halt—and who doesn't want to be more effective with this important tool? Plus, it is easy to do while you are seated at your desk, stuck in a meeting, or waiting for a child to finish her dance class.

A sturdy, hard-backed chair works best, but if you are thoughtful about your position and intensity, you can make nearly any chair work. Move to the front edge of the chair until your knees are at about a 90-degree angle and you are balancing equally on both seat bones. Keep your feet flat on the floor, about hip-width apart, and your shoulders stacked over your hips.

Take a deep inhale and simultaneously engage your abdominal core and the muscles of your inner thigh, drawing your knees toward each other. Be sure to keep your feet flat on the ground. Hold this engagement for a count of 10, with a steady breath, then slowly release back to neutral (figs. 6.6 A & B). Take a few cleansing breaths, then repeat this process four more times. As the effort becomes easier, add additional repetitions, until you can do 10 Seated Adductor Squeezes in a row.

*Scan to View Video*

**6.6 A & B** | Tami performs the Seated Adductor Squeeze, which is easy to do while seated at your desk, stuck in a meeting, or anytime where you are seated with time to get a mini workout! Start by keeping your legs about hips-width apart and your shoulders stacked over your hips. 6.6 B On the inhale, Tami engages her abdominal core and the muscles of her inner thigh, drawing her knees toward each other.

7

# Balance Challenges

From the first moment an Everyday Rider sets foot in the stirrup and swings her leg astride, she must work to master the art of appearing to be sitting still while mounted upon a moving horse. Ultimately, this comes down to developing the rider's ability to remain supple and balanced in her seat, with fluid, elastic, tension-free joints, in all gaits. Most would-be riders have little trouble balancing on a horse that is standing still. But as soon as he actually moves, the rider's ability to remain centered and stable is challenged in a myriad of ways. Riders must learn to activate new muscles, ligaments, and tendons, and improve their proprioceptive sense, to keep themselves centered over a constantly moving balance point. Much of what we teach a rider to do with her body—from maintaining the ear-shoulder-hip-heel alignment, to keeping the focal point up and forward, to feeling her weight evenly distributed over both seat bones—has to do with creating a condition in which it is possible for her to maintain balance (fig 7.1).

As an Everyday Rider spends more time in the saddle, develops a steadier position, and progresses in her skill building, her ability to balance on her horse gets better and better. Where a beginner may become unseated if her

**7.1** | From the first moment a rider sets foot in the stirrup, she must master the art of appearing to be sitting still while mounted upon a moving horse. Aria has developed her skills so she is able to remain centered and stable at all gaits. The Equicize exercises can aid riders in this effortless "look." Aria rides on the Albion College Equestrian Team in Albion, Michigan.

horse simply stumbles, a more experienced rider is able to quickly regain her balance even if the horse takes an unexpected spin. As she gains experience, the rider's ability to respond to balance challenges becomes almost instinctive.

So far, most of our Equicize exercises have focused on improving muscle strength, flexibility, and/or coordination, with just a pinch of balance challenge thrown in. All these important aspects of fitness help improve an athlete's ability to balance. But the following Equicize exercises are designed to put a rider's ability to balance to the test. If at first your balance doesn't receive a passing grade, then these exercises are the perfect "study buddy" to help bring up your average.

# Balance Challenge #1: Pommel Stands on an Increasing Count

Back in chapter 5 (p. 64), I introduced you to the Hip-Forward Pencil Stand, a component of the mounted Equicize warm-up (p. 69). In doing this exercise, you learned how to bring your body's balance forward over the pommel, and to use the engagement of your calves, quadriceps, and abdominal core to help hold your body ahead of the horse's center of balance for an extended period of time. This is a challenging balance point to maintain, because in nearly every other activity we do on horseback (including posting or sitting trot, light seat, and two-point), our goal is to maintain our center over the horse's "center," which is closely aligned with the seat of our saddle. Further, because the rider holds her Hip-Forward Pencil Stand for an increasing duration, she will especially feel the deepening stretch into her heels and the release of her hip flexors as she presses them forward.

In a Pommel Stand, the rider will move into a position similar to the Hip Forward Pencil Stand, but instead of fully opening the hip angle and pressing the pelvis forward, she will find her balance over the pommel with a more neutral hip. This slight modification in position emphasizes balance over strength and makes the rider's position more mobile—both qualities she will need to perform Pommel Stands on an increasing count. This exercise is a dynamic balance challenge and will both increase cardiovascular output and further test the rider's ability to reestablish her center (fig. 7.2).

Before you begin, it may be helpful to review pages 69–70, in which I describe the required alignment and positioning for the Hip Forward Pencil Stand. Again, the critical difference in Pommel Stand is the slightly more neutral hip angle. Instead of trying to hold your Stand position for as long as possible, now you will be alternating between Pommel Stand and posting trot on a consistent, rhythmical count. And unlike the Leg Builders (p. 76), which you practice on a decreasing count, here you will be adding beats to each sequence.

To get started, ask your horse for the rising trot. Stretch deeply through the heel, slide your leg into Power Leg, and rise into a Pommel Stand. Hold for two counts (think: "stand, two"), then post for three (count: "post, two, three"). Repeat this pattern for one circuit. When you return to your starting point, begin to stay in Pommel

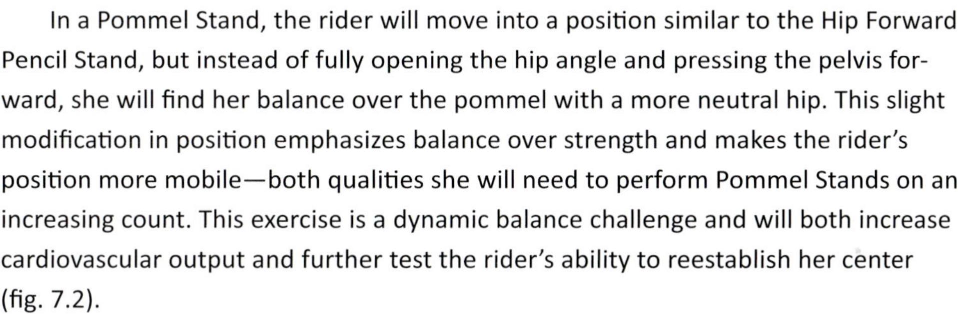

7.2 | Marianne is keeping her hip angle slightly more neutral in her Pommel Stand than she would if she were performing a Hip-Forward Pencil Stand. The Pommel Stand emphasizes balance over strength.

Stand for one additional count. This means you will hold the Pommel Stand for three counts ("stand, two, three"), then post for three counts. Do not worry about your posting diagonal during this exercise! Complete one circuit of "threes," then continue to build until you can also do a circuit of fours, and then fives.

Even if you found the warm-up variation of Hip-Forward Pencil Stand fairly easy, most riders find that the increased cardiovascular effort caused by transitioning between standing and posting makes this exercise a challenge. At first, it is riders who possess an innate sense of rhythm that are usually most successful in executing this exercise. For the rest of us—well, it can be a struggle in the beginning! If you find you are having trouble establishing a steady rhythm, or difficulty in holding your body in the Pommel Stand for the correct number of beats, I recommend playing music with a strong two-beat rhythm. Following the beat of a song played from the barn stereo or your phone seems to be just the cue that even the least rhythmical rider needs to find her center. Plus, music makes everything more fun!

## Balance Challenge #2: Two-Point Toe Touches

For an intense Balance Challenge, I recommend Two-Point Toe Touches. The ultimate expression of this exercise is performed in the trot, but for many riders, practicing Two-Point Toe Touches at the halt will be more than enough effort. Regardless of your fitness level and flexibility, I always recommend riders try this exercise at the halt first before moving on to the walk, then the trot.

*Scan to View Video*

Begin by sliding into Power Leg and establishing your balanced two-point position. Transfer both reins into your outside hand, then place your free inside hand onto your inside knee. Without losing the alignment of your hips over the seat of the saddle, slowly slide your inside hand down your leg until you are touching your shin, then your ankle, and maybe eventually, your toe (fig. 7.3). Hold for a two count, then return to center on a two count. Repeat 10 times, then change direction and do the same thing on the other side. As you complete each Toe Touch, keep your movements slow and steady; changing positions too quickly usually causes riders to lose their centered alignment over the saddle, and to use momentum instead of strength to move their body.

**7.3** | Marianne performs the Two-Point Toe Touches by placing both reins into her left hand and going up into her two-point. She slowly slides her hand down her leg until she is touching her toe, holds for a count of two, then returns to two-point. When doing the Toe Touches for the first time, it's a good idea to do it at the halt or walk, and if you need a modifier just reach slightly below the knee.

Riders should practice Two-Point Toe Touches at the halt until they feel fairly balanced and stable. Next, practice at the walk before trying the trot. As a rider gets stronger and better balanced, she can further modify upward by adding an additional set of 10 repetitions in each direction.

Two-Point Toe Touches will not only challenge your balance, but also increase the stretch on the backside of your legs, your extended arm, and your shoulder. If this action exceeds your level of "good stretch," modify by doing the exercise out of the Chest Press instead (p. 78).

Finally, the intensity of this balance challenge is not for everyone. If you find the action of reaching toward your toe to be too challenging, modify by extending your arm to the point at which you reach your personal edge. And, of course, if you ever feel that you have stretched so far that you are truly going to fall off, slow down a gait (or two!), or skip the exercise altogether.

# The Stair-Stepping Sashay

Just like their equine partners, most Everyday Riders have one side that is dominant. This means that when it comes to athletic performance, it is usually easier to do things with our dominant limbs, and we will unconsciously favor them under most circumstances. For example, if your phone falls off the counter, you will likely try to catch it with your dominant hand.

One everyday activity that most of us do, either at work or at home, is climb stairs. If you are able-bodied, this is probably an action you do completely automatically. But the next time you encounter a staircase, I want you to pause midway through the first step and notice which leg is leading, and which one is on the ground. Odds are good that you will have a preferred leg for stepping onto, and a preferred leg for pushing your body forward and up. When it comes time to descend the stairs, pause again and assess. Do you still want to lead with the same leg? Or have your legs switched positions?

The Stair-Stepping Sashay is an easy way to develop greater symmetry in movement, to increase muscle strength in the weaker limb, and to improve your brain-body coordination. Once you have identified your preferred method of climbing up and down the stairs, consciously switch the roles of each leg. It sounds simple, but I guarantee that overcoming years of unconscious movement is not all that easy to do!

If ascending and descending full sets of stairs is not part of your usual routine, you can still get a similar benefit from this simple variation. Using a single step or your mounting block, step

7.4 | **Work your non-dominant leg by performing the Stair Stepping Sashay. Most of us have a dominant side and prefer to lead when taking steps or hiking with one leg over the other. Practice using your non-dominant side by stepping up stairs with your non-dominant leg.**

up leading with your left foot, bring your right foot to join, then step down leading with the left foot, followed by the right (fig. 7.4). Repeat these steps 10 times, pause, then start over—this time leading with your right foot, followed by the left.

Other everyday leg symmetry actions to notice include becoming aware of how you prefer to sit or stand. For example, if you sit cross-legged on the ground, you will instinctively place one leg in front and the other behind. Try to become conscious of which limb wants to be where and choose to switch their positions from time to time. When you stand in line, do you tend to cock one hip and weight one leg more than the other? This posture can become habitual, and so by concentrating on standing centered over both feet, you can improve both your symmetry and coordination in the saddle.

# Achilles Stretches

I don't think there is an Everyday Rider out there who has not received the following feedback from her instructor: "Get your heels DOWN!" Keeping your weight toward the heel and maintaining a position in which the heel is lower than the toe is an essential component to creating a correct, balanced alignment in nearly every equestrian discipline. But this is not a posture we routinely adopt under any other circumstance—not in sports, and certainly not in our daily lives.

For these reasons, many riders struggle with restriction in their Achilles, a particularly fibrous tendon that connects the calf muscle to the heel. The Achilles plays an important role in our bipedal mobility, and as such it is strong more than it is flexible. Forcing an Achilles stretch can result in a serious injury called a rupture, which may require surgery to repair. Consistent, gentle stretching of this important tendon is the best way to protect it from injury.

To keep your Achilles healthy while also preparing it for the less-than-natural

**7.5 A** | Tami performs the Everyday Equicize Achilles Stretch on the mounting block step. This Stair Stretch closely replicates the type of feeling riders get in their calves while in the saddle. Simply find a step, place the ball of your foot on the edge, and hang your heel down.

position we adopt while in the saddle, consider adding some of the following Everyday Equicize Achilles Stretches to your daily activities:

The Stair Stretch: This exercise is probably the one most frequently recommended by instructors, because it so closely replicates the type of feeling we get in our calves and Achilles while in the saddle. Simply find a stair, place the balls of your feet on the edge with your heels hanging off the step, and lower your weight down (fig. 7.5 A). You can do this one heel at a time, or both at once. Whichever option you choose, use the wall or banister for stability. Hold the stretch smoothly for a count of five (no bouncing), then release. Repeat five times.

The Wall Stretch: Some riders find the Stair Stretch too intense; if this is you, or if you live in a single-story dwelling, the Wall Stretch is a great alternative (fig. 7.5 B). There are two variations, so choose the one that works best for you.

For Wall Stretch Variation #1, flex the ankle and place the toes and ball of foot against the base of a wall. Drop your weight toward the heel of the flexed foot and lean against the wall with your arms until you feel a stretch in the calf and Achilles. Hold for a count of five, release, and repeat five times, then switch feet.

For Wall Stretch Variation #2, place your feet about hip-width apart from

7.5 B | Tami performs the Wall Stretch in order to stretch her calves and Achilles. Here, Tami keeps her feet hips-width apart, stands about 3 feet from the wall, leans forward until she feels the stretch, then holds it for a count of five.

each other, and about 3 feet away from the wall. Reach your arms forward and lean against the wall, keeping your feet flat on the floor with the toes pointed forward, until you feel a stretch in your calves. Play with the distance your feet are placed from the wall until you find the spacing that creates "good stretch" in your body. Again, hold for a count of five, release, and repeat five times.

It is also easy to add a quick but effective Achilles stretch into your daily routine at the barn—this is especially useful on a cold day, or if you are someone who simply feels like you have restriction in your calves upon mounting. Using a squared-off cavaletti pole, or even the mounting block, place your toes and the ball of your foot on the edge and let your heel hang down, just as you would in the Stair Stretch (see fig. 7.4 A). Hold for a count of five, release, and repeat, then change sides.

Again, it is important to remember that pain is not the goal. If at any point in these stretches, you experience pain in the joints of your feet or ankle, or in the soft tissues that support these joints, stop immediately and seek medical advice.

# Upper Body and Arm Builders

**W**hen it comes to perfecting rider position, much of our focus goes toward the legs and seat, and with good reason—it is only when our legs and seat are properly positioned and secure that we can effectively use these aids to communicate with the horse (fig. 8.1). But as a rider progresses, she will learn that to be truly effective, she needs to use her entire body in a coordinated manner to produce the results she wants from the horse. Riding well isn't just about using the arms to stop and the legs to go. The rider must also engage her back and abdominal muscles and use the influence of the weight and angle of her torso to help achieve better downward transitions, lighten a horse off the forehand, or regain control of a horse that has lost his balance on a turn, for just a few examples. I discuss many of the ways in which riders can effectively use their biomechanics to achieve these outcomes in my book *The Athletic Equestrian*.

For a rider to effectively use the upper body and arms to support her horse, the muscles, ligaments, and tendons surrounding these areas need to be toned and flexible. In my years of teaching, I have found that riders tend to have strong biceps, which is the muscle located on the front side of the

## BICEPS OR BICEP? A SHORT GRAMMATICAL LESSON

The word "biceps" literally means "two-headed," referring to the fact that this is a muscle with two "heads," or attachments, to bone. "Biceps" is of Latin origin, and you hear a similar ending (-ceps) in the names of other muscles, including the triceps and quadriceps. Can you guess how many attachments these muscles have?

In English, it is unusual for a singular noun to have an "s" at the end, and it has become common for speakers to simply say "bicep" when referring to this muscle. However, "biceps" is most correct, scientifically speaking, and this is why we have chosen to use it here.

upper arm. This is probably because so many of our daily horse chores—lifting buckets, moving jumps, even restraining a strong horse in hand—require us to engage this muscle (figs. 8.2 A & B). But the biceps is just one of the many muscles that help to control our arms and upper back, and we need all of them to be working in unison to ride effectively.

Equicize includes a series of six Upper Body and Arm Builders that comprehensively work not only the biceps, but the deltoids, the trapezius, the pectorals, and more. These exercises are designed to not just build strength but also improve suppleness and elasticity and increase

8.2 A & B | Through my years teaching, I have found riders tend to have strong biceps through their everyday chores like carrying buckets (A). Riders like Phoebe also get strong biceps from moving around jumps and even holding a strong horse in hand (B). However, riders need to improve strength in all their arm, shoulder, and back muscles.

**8.3** | Ideally, I like my riders to perform all six of the arm exercises in the **two-point position to get an increased workout. Try to find your personal edge and remember that your edge may change from workout to workout.**

range of motion. Additionally, any exercise in which your arms are held at shoulder-height or higher also increases your cardiovascular output. If you don't believe me, simply walk around your house as normal, then elevate your arms above your head, and retrace your steps—you will find you are breathing heavier and faster with your arms up.

Just as with our previous Equicize exercises, experiment with the Upper Body and Arm Builders at the halt or walk at first, before moving onto the posting trot. The ultimate upward modifier for this sequence is to complete all six exercises at the trot while holding the two-point position (fig. 8.3).

I will be honest—for most riders, being able to perform the Upper Body and Arm Builders at the walk or posting trot is hard enough work. Do not get discouraged in any way if the thought of doing a Boxer Punch or Under-Arm Popeye in the two-point at the trot seems impossible. Additionally, for all riders, it is to be expected that some arm exercises will be easier than others. You may be able to perform some exercises at the posting trot, but still need to return to the walk for the rest. As always, try to find your personal edge, and remember that your edge can change from workout to workout.

*Scan to View Video*

When I teach the Upper Body and Arm Builder sequence, I usually have riders do all six exercises with one arm, then switch and do them with the opposite side. But if you find your arm turns to jelly halfway through, you may find better success by changing rein after every two or three exercises to work the opposite arm. Initially, aim to complete a set of 10 for each exercise on each arm. As your fitness increases and time allows, build to completing two or even three sets of 10 on each side, for each exercise.

## Upper Body and Arm Builder #1: Popeye

If you are familiar with the old-time cartoon character "Popeye," you will already have a good idea of what this exercise is about! Popeye is a sailor who develops super strength when he eats a can of spinach, and he is always willing to show off his flexed biceps. In this Upper Body and Arm Builder, you will be adopting a position that will show off your flexed biceps, just like Popeye.

*Scan to View Video*

# Arm Weights

For many Everyday Riders, the Upper Body and Arm Builder sequence will be a challenge to complete at the walk or posting trot, at least at first. But if you remain dedicated and committed to practicing these exercises at least a few times per week, you should begin to feel stronger and more capable. When you get to the point that the exercises feel easy, and they no longer produce significant fatigue (which is sometimes only made apparent the next day, in the form of sore muscles), adding arm weights can be the perfect upward modifier.

For Equicize, I prefer the style of arm weight that slips over the wrist and is secured with Velcro. Keep your arm weights ringside, and when you reach this stage of your Equicize routine, just slide them on. There is no need to choose the heaviest weights available—a 1- or 2-pound weight will be more than sufficient to add intensity to each movement (fig. 8.4).

Some Everyday Riders have also found benefit in using arm weights during other segments of the Equicize routine, such as the Two-Point Toe Touches or One-Handed Chest Press. As you become more confident and secure in the routine, and feel fitter overall, consider arm weights to be an optional added challenge to help build greater strength and increase cardiovascular output.

8.4 | Arm weights are an upward modifier for all your Equicize arm exercises once you need to add a little more "oomph" to your arm workouts!

Begin tracking left. Transfer your reins into your outside (right) hand. With your
free inside (left) hand, make a fist and extend your arm straight out to your left side
at shoulder height, knuckles facing up. Contract your biceps, bending your elbow until
the knuckles of your fist are resting on your rotator cuff muscles and tendons or collar
bone. Be sure to keep the elbow lifted to shoulder height; your upper arm should
be pointing straight out to the side, held even with your shoulder and parallel to the
ground. This is the starting position for Popeye (fig. 8.5 A).

8.5 A | Marianne has transferred her reins into her left hand and performs the *Popeye* by making a fist with her other hand and extending her arm straight out to the side at shoulder-height.

From the starting position, keep your elbow lifted so it is even with your shoulder, then open the elbow joint until your arm is once again extended, with the knuckles of your fist facing the sky (figs. 8.5 B & C).  Now, smoothly bend the lower arm back into the starting position, knuckles touching your rotator cuff or collar bone. Repeat this sequence 10 times.

Sometimes, riders get a bit carried away doing Popeye, and they rapidly flail their arm up and down. Although that may be fun, you will receive greater benefit doing Popeye—and the other Upper Body and Arm Builders—in a steady and methodical rhythm. I coach riders to count "one-and, two-and," with the number being the extension, "and" being the retraction.

8.5 B & C | After the arm is fully extended, Marianne contracts her bicep and bends her elbow until the knuckles of her fist are resting on her rotator cuff muscles and tendons (B). Tami performs the Popeye and repeats it 10 times with each arm (C).

8.6 A | Morgan performs the Under-Arm Popeye by extending her arm straight out from the shoulder but brings the clenched fist in toward her armpit rather than on top by her rotator cuff. Here, she has slightly over-rotated her wrist and her knuckles face back instead of down.

## Upper Body and Arm Builder #2: Under-Arm Popeye

After completing the Popeye exercise, the Under-Arm Popeye will work the opposing sets of muscles.

Set up with your reins in the outside (right) hand and inside (left) arm extended straight out from the shoulder, left hand held in a soft fist. This time, hold your fist knuckles down, and when you bend the elbow, draw the fist and your lower arm toward your armpit on the same side. Keep your elbow lifted, and your upper arm at least even with your shoulder. This is the starting position for Under-Arm Popeye (fig. 8.6 A).

From the starting position, first extend your lower arm back out to the side, parallel to the ground and knuckles facing down. Second, bend the elbow, keeping

*Scan to View Video*

**8.6 B** | After Morgan brings her arm in by bending at the elbow, she extends it straight again, making sure to keep it at shoulder-height. She does 10 repetitions, then does the same exercise with the other arm.

the upper arm lifted and even with the shoulder, drawing your fist back toward your armpit (fig. 8.6 B). Repeat this sequence smoothly and methodically 10 times.

This exercise activates the deltoid muscles supporting your shoulder, and many riders feel its effects more quickly and more intensely than Popeye. As you begin to feel the effort of the exercise, maintain your steady breath and rhythm of movement, and be sure to keep your elbow lifted and upper arm even with your shoulder.

## Upper Body and Arm Builder #3: Stop Sign

With Stop Sign, riders channel their "inner crossing guard" while also toning their triceps (which run along the back of the upper arm), and their pectorals (along the upper chest).

*Scan to View Video*

**8.7 A** | Reina performs the Stop Sign, which tones her triceps as well as her pectorals. She has put both reins in her left hand, extends her right arm straight out to the side with the hand open and the palm facing forward, then bends the elbow until it is at a 90-degree angle.

With the reins in your outside (right) hand, extend your inside (left) arm straight out to the side, in line with your shoulder, hand open and palm facing forward. While still keeping the upper arm even with the shoulder, bend the left elbow until it is at a 90-degree angle, lifting your open palm up. Your elbow is now essentially making an "L" shape. This is your starting position for Stop Sign (fig 8.7 A).

From the starting position, keep the upper arm stable while folding the forearm forward. Stop when the forearm is parallel to the ground, and on the same plane as the upper arm and shoulder. It will look almost as if the "L" is lying down (figs. 8.7 B & C). Return to the starting position.

Repeat Stop Sign 10 times. Be sure to keep the upper arm in line with the shoulder and the shoulders down and away from your ears, all while moving your lower arm in a smooth, rhythmical manner.

8.7 B & C | Reina keeps the upper arm stable, then folds the forearm forward, stopping when the forearm is parallel to the ground and on the same plane as the upper arm and shoulder (B). Tami performs the Stop Sign at Dartmouth Riding Center at The Morton Farm in Etna, New Hampshire (C).

## Upper Body and Arm Builder #4: Chicken Wing

*Scan to View Video*

If you have ever danced the "Funky Chicken" at a wedding (and even if you haven't), based on the name alone, you might have a guess in regard to the required arm position for this exercise! The Chicken Wing challenges the suppleness of the rider's shoulder joint and offers a great stretch for the triceps.

Place your reins into the outside (right) hand and extend the inside (left) arm out to the side, in line with the shoulder, palm facing up. Bend the left elbow and place your fingertips on your rotator cuff, collar bone, or the back of your neck. You will be holding the fingers in this position for the entire exercise, so place them wherever they are most comfortable (fig. 8.8 A). Congratulations—you now have a Chicken Wing!

8.8 A | **Amanda performs the Chicken Wing by bending her elbow and placing her fingertips on her rotator cuff. You can also place your fingertips on your collar bone or the back of your neck.**

8.8 B & C | Keeping her elbow straight out, Amanda than engages the muscles of her upper arm and lifts the elbow until the point of the elbow is nearly straight up and her biceps is along her ear (B). Tami performs 10 repetitions of the Chicken Wing before changing arms and doing 10 repetitions with the opposite arm (C).

While maintaining this position, engage the muscles of your upper arm and lift the left elbow until the point of your elbow is nearly straight up, and your biceps is alongside your ear (figs 8.8 B & C). Hold for a beat, then lower to the starting position—upper arm even with your shoulder, elbow pointing to the left side. Repeat 10 times.

Chicken Wing, despite its silly name, is seriously hard work. Even when the arm is in the starting or "resting" position, the muscles of your upper arm will still be working. Depending on the elasticity of the soft tissue in your shoulder and upper arm, it might not be possible to point the elbow straight up, or to bring the biceps even with your ear. Simply do your best, and work to bring the arm a little closer to this position as you continue to practice the exercise.

## Upper Body and Arm Builder #5: Boxer Punches



Boxer Punches will give you a chance to work out any pent-up frustrations, in a healthy and strength-building way! Just as the name implies, in this exercise the rider will move through the mechanics of a punch in the air—but hopefully, no actual fighting will be involved.

To execute a Boxer Punch, start yet again by putting both reins into your outside (right) hand. Make a soft fist with the left hand and bend the left elbow until your fist is at your nose (almost as if you were punching yourself), with the point of your elbow aiming out in front of you (fig. 8.9 A). This is the starting position for the Boxer Punch.

8.9 A | Marianne performs the Boxer Punches, perfect for working out some pent-up frustrations! She makes a fist and bends her elbow until her fist is at her nose.

**8.9 B | Marianne performs the second part of the Boxer Punch by keeping her elbow lifted and snapping the arm forward as if she is throwing a punch into the air.**

While trying to keep your left elbow lifted, snap the left arm forward as if you were throwing a punch into the air. You rotate the forearm as you extend it, so the palm side of the fist ends up facing down. Put some force into the punch, as if you were actually hitting something (fig. 8.9 B). Return to the starting position and repeat 10 times.

## Upper Body and Arm Builder #6: Victory Punches

The Victory Punch is the perfect finale exercise to celebrate completing the Equicize Upper Body and Arm Builder sequence. But instead of imagining we are striking something in front of us, as in the Boxer Punch, Victory Punches see us directing that energy up and into the sky.

After transferring your reins into the outside (right) hand, make a soft fist with the left hand, extend your arm out to the left side, and bend your elbow until it makes an "L," the knuckles of your fist facing up. This is your starting position for the Victory Punch (fig. 8.10 A). Throw your punch by forcefully opening your elbow and extending your left arm into the air, rotating the lower arm to add emphasis to the punch (fig. 8.10B). Return to the starting position and repeat 10 times.

One important note for both the Boxer and Victory Punches—it is easiest for most riders if they coordinate the in-and-out movements of the punch with the beats of their post in the trot. For example, the arm is in the resting position during the sitting beat, and in the extended or "punching" position in the rising beat. Be sure to keep your core engaged, especially in the Victory Punches, to help you remain centered.

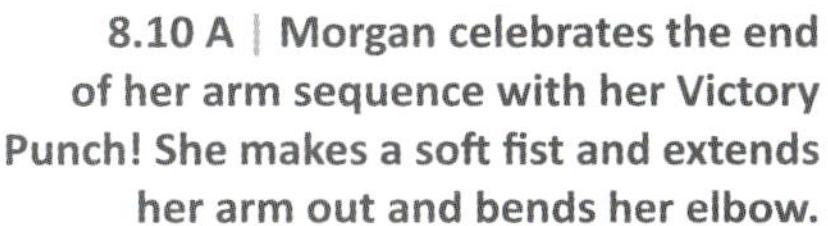

8.10 A | Morgan celebrates the end of her arm sequence with her Victory Punch! She makes a soft fist and extends her arm out and bends her elbow.

**8.10 B** | Morgan "throws" her punch by opening her elbow and extending her arm into the air, rotating the lower arm to add emphasis to the punch.

# Computer Tension Release Sequence

**M**eeting the demands of today's digital world means that, more than ever, much of our unmounted time is likely spent sitting at a desk. As we concentrate on our work, studies, social media, and other digital pursuits, it is quite easy to acquire negative physical habits that come back to haunt us in the saddle. If you have ever struggled to stay tall with your upper body, to keep your shoulders down and back, or to keep your eyes up and ahead, this is likely part of the reason why. Even more troubling, when we habitually hold our bodies in a slumped, collapsed, or hunched position, it can lead to pain and repetitive-use injuries (fig. 8.11).

The good news is that with conscious attention, it is possible to practice positive posture instead. First, make sure that the setup of your desk is ergonomically correct: your device should be positioned so it is easy and comfortable to maintain a tall posture, with shoulders stacked over hips and eyes focused forward. If you don't know how to do this, there are some excellent references available online, or consult your medical professional or physiotherapist.

But even when we are holding positive posture, the stress of our day can still wear on us. When you feel tension coming on—or perhaps it is just that low point of the day when your energy is waning—try a Computer Tension Release Sequence. This easy two-step sequence helps to stretch the upper body and rejuvenate your energy.

Start by centering yourself, either in athletic stance (if you are standing) or on your seat bones

8.11 | Much of our unmounted time is spent at a desk, usually in front of a computer. This can lead to upper bodies that are slumped with the shoulders collapsed.

8.12 | Tami releases tension in her upper body by doing the first of the Computer Tension Release Sequence. She takes her right arm and draws it across her upper chest, placing her left hand on the right elbow or upper arm, and holds it for a count of five, then switches arms.

8.13 | Tami then lifts both shoulders up toward her ears and rolls them backward until the shoulder blades fall down her back. She repeats this five to 10 times, coming back to neutral each time.

at the edge of your chair, feet flat on the floor and placed about hip-width apart. Take your right arm and draw it across your upper chest, placing your left hand on the right elbow or upper arm, whichever feels more comfortable (fig. 8.12). Using your left hand, apply gentle pressure until you feel a good stretch in the muscles of your upper arm, shoulder, and upper back. Hold this cross-body stretch for a count of five, then switch arms. Repeat until you have done this stretch with each arm three times.

Return to your centered position. Lift both of your shoulders up into your ears, then slowly and deliberately roll them backward until the shoulder blades fall down your back (fig. 8.13). Most people report feeling a lovely "tingling" sensation, almost as if they are getting a shoulder massage! Repeat this motion between five and seven times, always rolling the shoulders back and down, never forward. This will help to release the muscles of the upper back and open the chest and serves as the perfect pick-me-up.

# Toning Your Core

As I have previously discussed elsewhere in this book, to be effective, the Everyday Rider must be able to give smooth and coordinated cues to her mount, all while remaining balanced, centered, and supple astride a powerful, mobile creature. So far in our Equicize sequence, we have challenged the rider's arms, legs, torso, upper body, and balance (fig. 9.1). But what you might not have immediately noticed is that to successfully complete any of the previous exercises, the rider has also been (perhaps unconsciously) engaging her core.

When coaches refer to the rider's core, they are talking about a collection of muscles located deep within the abdomen and lower back. Collectively, these muscles support the spine and pelvis and aid in the stability of the rider's trunk. Each muscle plays a specific role but fulfills its duties best when used in harmonious concert with the other core muscles. A rider with a "toned core" usually demonstrates a high degree of balance, steadiness, and security in the saddle. This, in turn, leads to confidence, and the ability to use her limbs independently.

I think we can agree that developing a toned core is a key stepping stone on the path toward becoming an effective rider. Unfortunately for most of us,

9.1 | A rider with a toned core usually demonstrates a high degree of balance, steadiness, and security in the saddle. This, in turn, leads to confidence and the ability to use her limbs independently.

thanks to desk jobs or other daily commitments that keep us sedentary, we are not quite as toned in our core as would be ideal. But if you hear the expression "toning your core" and are immediately filled with visions of an agonizing sequence of sit ups, planks, and crab kicks—take a deep breath, because Equicize includes none of those. Instead, we are going to utilize two simple exercises—Gluteal Squeezes and Abdominal Squeezes—to help riders regain awareness of these body parts and to add fitness to these critical muscle groups.

Both Gluteal and Abdominal Squeezes are performed at the posting trot. As with any of the Equicize exercises, you can always modify to practice them at the walk or halt instead. But as you read through this chapter, I encourage you to try your first Gluteal or Abdominal Squeezes right where you are sitting. Trust me—even as an instructor, I can't "see" the rider perform either of these exercises, so no one sitting near you will be any the wiser. The muscular engagement is completely internal, with external results only becoming evident over time, as the rider's toned core allows her to develop increased stability and coordination in the saddle.

To get started, I will explain the required muscular engagement for first the Gluteal Squeeze, then the Abdominal Squeeze. Next, because each exercise requires awareness of similar position cues and challenges, I will discuss those concepts together. Finally, I will explain how to combine these two unique actions into one sequence that will help riders successfully develop increased awareness and tone in their core.

First up—the Gluteal Squeeze.

Okay riders, here I have to level with you. Without getting overly scientific and technical, there is no "delicate" way of naming the part of your anatomy involved with the Gluteal Squeezes. Whatever your favorite nickname for the trio of gluteal muscles may be—bum, buns, cheeks, hindquarter, backside, derriere, etcetera—you are going to squeeze those muscles together, hold, and then release (fig. 9.2).

In the Abdominal Squeeze, the rider contracts her abdominal muscles, hold this contraction, then releases. Most of us have some sense of what is meant by the abdominal core, but I always remind riders to begin their Abdominal Squeeze by imagining they are pulling their belly button up and in, toward their spine (fig. 9.3). This action usually ensures the rider is engaging the appropriate abdominal muscle groups.

*Scan to View Video*

9.2 | Although difficult to see in photos, Gluteal Squeezes are a great exercise to help tone your entire core and are performed at the halt, walk, or posting trot.

9.3 | In the Abdominal Squeeze, Marianne contracts her abdominal muscles by imagining she is pulling her belly button up and in toward her spine. She then holds it for a count of 10 at the halt, walk, or posting trot.

While engaging either one of these muscle groups seems easy enough to do, the hard part comes with making sure that other, supporting muscle groups don't get involved too. For example, most riders will struggle at first to perform the Gluteal Squeeze without also engaging their thighs; when performing the Abdominal Squeeze, riders often collapse or round the upper body. For both types of Squeezes, the rider needs to maintain her traditional ear-shoulder-hip-heel alignment, and focus on only squeezing either the glutes or the abdominal core, while keeping the other muscles around them neutral and relaxed.

Astute readers likely will recognize that engaging these muscle groups is also part of the coordinated sequence of aids used to execute a smooth downward transition.

*Scan to View Video*



# Gluteal and Abdominal Squeezes

Yes, you read that correctly! This Everyday Equicize option is exactly the same as the actual mounted version. Because it is almost impossible to tell when someone is activating their glutes or their abdominal core just by looking at them, Everyday Riders can practice their Squeezes almost anytime and anywhere. Zoning out during a meeting? Practice an Abdominal Squeeze. Sitting in your car at a stoplight (fig. 9.4)? Hold a Gluteal Squeeze while you wait for the light to change. These easy-to-achieve Equicizes are the perfect option to tone your core, both on and off your horse!

9.4 | Riders can practice their Glute and Abdominal Squeezes anywhere—while sitting in a meeting, waiting for an elevator, or sitting in the car at a red light.

When an Everyday Rider begins practicing the Squeezes, often she will find her horse slows down, from trot to walk or even walk to a halt. If your horse is getting confused, be prepared to close your lower leg to motivate him forward once again. Most horses figure out pretty quickly that when their rider does this exercise, she is not actually asking for a downward transition. It is perhaps only the laziest of mounts who continues to take advantage and slows down in response to his rider's Squeezes; in this case, it might be best to simply practice the exercise only at the walk.

After experimenting with your Squeezes in the walk, establish a positive forward posting trot. Now, you will coordinate each Squeeze for a specific count. Start with the Gluteal Squeeze, holding the engagement for a count of 10 posting strides (with each up-down equaling a count of "one"). When you reach 10, relax your muscles, and post as normal for a few strides to reset. Next, activate your Abdominal Squeeze, again holding the engagement for a count of 10 posting strides. Continue alternating between the two Squeezes for two full circuits.

As you get fitter, you should be able to gradually increase the number of successive circuits you can complete of alternating Gluteal and Abdominal Squeezes. You will know it is time to increase the challenge when completing two full circuits doesn't significantly elevate your heart and respiratory rates, and both of these vital signs quickly return to normal after you release the muscle engagement. As you add circuits, be sure to maintain your form, and to keep your breath steady.

# Cell Phone Torso Twist

Back in chapter 5 (p. 64), when I discussed the Equicize mounted warm-up, I introduced you to the Mounted Torso Twist (p. 66). The Cell Phone Torso Twist takes that same movement and turns it into an Everyday Equicize option, perfect to practice whenever you find yourself chatting on the phone.

Stand with your feet hip-width apart; keep your knees soft and your pelvis facing squarely forward. It is important to remember that the Twist should happen in your waist, not your hips and lower back. It can be helpful to keep your free hand resting on the point of hip on the same side, just to be sure the pelvis isn't trying to turn when you rotate the upper body.

If you are holding the phone in your right hand and up to your right ear, start by twisting your upper body to the left (figs. 9.5 A & B). Hold for a count of five, then bring your torso back to center. Recheck the alignment of your pelvis. Switch the phone to your opposite (left) hand and ear, then twist to the right.

When you are using ear buds or other hands-free devices, place both hands on the wings of your pelvis, and complete the twist as above.

*Scan to View Video*

**9.5 A & B** | Tami practices her Everyday Equicize Cell Phone Torso Twist by setting her hips square to the front, then twisting her body from the waist up all the way to her left (A). Tami has let her hips follow the twist, but you should try to keep your hips square for this exercise. Tami then continues her Cell Phone Twist by going neutral to the front, then twisting from the waist up all the way to her right (B).

# Cool Down

Most riders are familiar with the elements of a cool-down phase for their horse, whether it is completed by offering a stretching circle at the trot, a long-rein stretch at the walk, or taking a quiet hack around a field. The cool-out phase allows the horse's heart and respiratory rates to slowly lower, the lactic acid to be flushed from exercised muscles, and the body's cooling mechanisms to help return the horse's temperature to normal. For all these same reasons, and because Equicize challenges riders to push themselves out of their physical comfort zones, it is important to pay a little extra attention to the Cool Down for the Everyday Rider's body as well (fig. 10.1).

Just because it is called the Cool Down doesn't mean no effort is involved—the Everyday Rider will still be working, but at a lower intensity. Imagine for a moment the process that a jockey uses when bringing a finely tuned racing Thoroughbred back at the end of a race. First, she slows from the gallop to the canter, then spends some time at the trot, before finally settling to the walk. In Equicize, the Everyday Rider will apply a similarly decreasing level of power and intensity to her movements as she comes to the end of her exercise sequence, helping to return both horse and rider to their baseline.

10.1 | **The cool-out phase allows both the horse's and rider's heart and respiratory rates to slowly lower and the lactic acid to be flushed from exercised muscles.**

The full Equicize Cool Down is most appropriate for the Everyday Rider who has built her fitness up to the point where she can do the entire Equicize sequence at the trot, with only occasional walk breaks (while always remaining mindful of her mount's fitness—see p. 16). In the Equicize Cool Down, riders revisit two previous exercises—the Two-Point/Chest Press (p. 77) and Sit-Ones (p. 73)—but this time, you do them in reverse, on an increasing count. You conclude your Equicize routine with one final new challenge—Mounted Push-Ups.

Throughout this book, I have emphasized the importance of riders finding their personal edge for any given exercise. The "edge" looks different for everyone, and it

**10.2 A** | Morgan begins the Chest Press/Two-Point in Reverse sequence by holding her Chest Press for a two-count.

may mean that an Everyday Rider can complete some, but not all, Equicize exercises at the trot. If you are not yet up to a level of fitness that permits you to complete all the previous exercises at the trot, or you returned to the walk to execute the last several exercises, you have already begun lowering the intensity of your workout. Therefore, skip the Two-Point/Chest Press and Sit-Ones in the Cool Down, and go directly to the Mounted Push-Ups for your final exercise.

## Cool Down #1: Chest Press/Two-Point in Reverse

Back in chapter 6 (p. 76), I introduced you to the Two-Point/Chest Press exercise as part of our Leg Builder sequence (p. 77). At that point in the workout, your goal was to build strength in your legs and to increase cardiovascular output by alternating between each position on a gradually shortening count. In your Cool Down, you are going to use the

**10.2 B | Morgan then transitions into two-point position for a count of two, repeating this pattern for half a circuit. She will then do a half circuit each on a three count, four count, and five count.**

same positions but instead of beginning with the Two-Point, you will start with the Chest Press—and instead of shortening the count, you will lengthen it, thereby allowing your breath and heart rate to stabilize, and helping to cool your muscles (figs. 10.2 A & B).

To get started, send your horse into a positive, forward posting trot. Establish your Power Leg (p. 32), move up into your two-point, then get into your Chest Press by bringing your chest to the horse's crest while sliding your hips back toward the cantle. Hold for a count of two, then transition back to two-point; hold for a count of two. Continue alternating between these two positions on a count of two for half a circuit of the arena. Next, hold each position for a count of three for half a circuit, then increase to a count of four for half a circuit, and finally conclude with half a circuit on a five count. Be sure to keep your breath even and steady as the count increases. Remember, the goal here is to help your body cool down and return to stasis—to do that, it will need oxygen!

## Cool Down #2: Sit-Ones in Reverse

In chapter 5 (p. 64), I detailed the components of the Mounted Equicize Warm-Up, which included Sit-Ones on a decreasing count. As a reminder, Sit-Ones challenge the Everyday Rider's ability to remain centered and balanced by deliberately following or resisting the movements of her horse's trot. In your Cool Down, you will revisit the Sit-Ones, but now on an increasing count. Most riders report feeling a greater degree of control and influence in the Sit-Ones during the Cool Down as opposed to their warm-up; in the Cool Down, Sit-Ones in Reverse also help riders to re-center their mind by coming back to a consistent and steady beat (fig. 10.3).

First, establish a positive forward posting trot. Choose a starting point on the edge

10.3 | Loretta cools down both her body and her horse's body by doing Sit-Ones in Reverse. She starts by sitting one in order to get on the opposite posting diagonal every two strides, then gradually works up to sitting one every five strides.

of your arena, then begin your Sit-Ones by posting for two beats, sitting for one beat, posting for two. Continue this pattern for half a circuit, then increase to posting for three beats, sitting for one, then posting for three. Again, repeat this pattern for half a circuit. Continue to increase by one posting beat for half a circuit each, until you have completed a half circuit of fours, then fives.

*Scan to View Video*

## Cool Down #3: Mounted Push-Ups

After completing the first two Cool Down exercises, return your horse to the walk, then bring him to the center of the arena and come to the halt. It is time to complete your final Equicize exercise—Mounted Push-Ups.

In a traditional push-up, the athlete begins in the plank position—balanced on her two hands, and either her toes or knees. She then engages her core and upper back, as well as the biceps, triceps, and deltoids, to lower her body to the ground, then pushes back up to her starting position. In contrast, for a Mounted Push-Up, all the effort should be in the arms, with almost no engagement of the muscles in the back or core (fig. 10.4).

Mounted Push-Ups are done from the two-point position. Until the Everyday Rider has figured out the specific mechanics of the Mounted Push-Up, she should remain halted,

10.4 | In traditional push-ups, the rider begins in the plank position and lowers her body to the ground, then pushes back up. In a Mounted Push-Up, all the effort should be in the arms with almost no engagement of the muscles in the back or core.

10.5 | Marianne demonstrates the Rope Climber Push-Up: she has stacked her fists and placed them on the horse's crest. This method of holding your hands works both the biceps and triceps.

with her feet in the stirrups. However, in my experience, many riders actually find it easier to do the Mounted Push-Up correctly—meaning they are relying only on their arms to move the upper body—without stirrups.

Mounted Push-Ups are performed in three sets of 10, with the hands placed in different positions for each set. The changes in hand position will help the rider to engage different arm muscles.

• **Hand Position #1**—Rope Climber: While keeping one rein in each hand (or both in one hand, if you are riding Western), make two soft fists. Stack your fists one on top of the other, almost as if you are climbing rope, then place them knuckle-side down about halfway up the horse's crest (fig. 10.5). Your thumbs face your body, and your elbows point out to each side. The Rope Climber works both the biceps and the triceps.

- **Hand Position #2**—The Butterfly: Spread your fingers open and overlap your thumbs, facing your palms away from your body, thumbs pointing toward the horse's ears. Continue to hold each rein between your ring finger and pinky and forefinger and thumb; it will drape between these two points, and rest against the horse's neck. Press your thumbs down halfway up the horse's crest, allowing the rest of your fingers to wrap on either side of the horse's neck for stability (fig. 10.6). This variation particularly challenges the biceps.

- **Hand Position #3**—Flat Hands: Open your fingers, continuing to loop the rein between your ring finger and pinky and forefinger and thumb, palms facing away from your body. Rotate your hands so both thumbs are pointing toward your chest, then place one hand above the other midway up the horse's crest. Allow the rest of your fingers to gently rest alongside the horse's crest (figs. 10.7 A & B). This variation is an excellent workout for the triceps.

10.6 | Tami demonstrates the Butterfly method of holding her hands for push-ups. She points her thumbs toward the horse's ears, which challenges her biceps.

 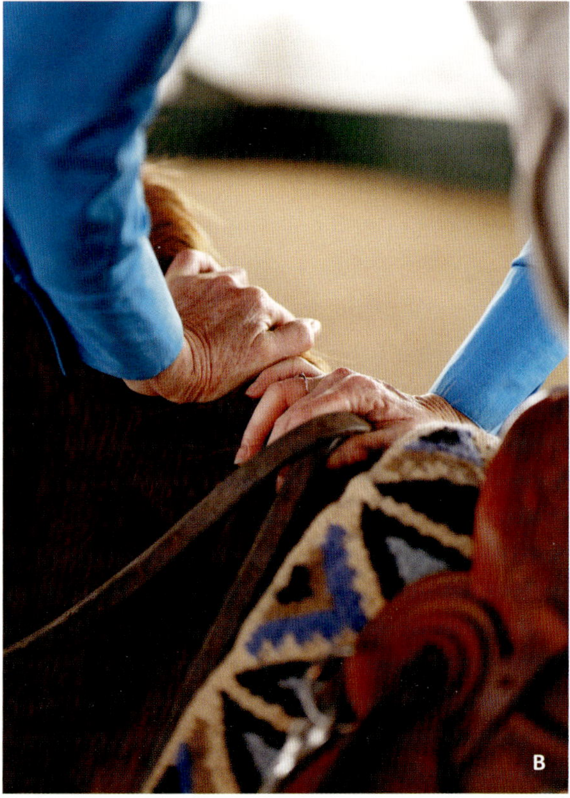

**10.7 A & B** | I'm demonstrating how to hold your hands in the Flat Hands position by showing how both thumbs point toward the saddle and rider (A). When Tami holds her hands in the Flat Hands position, it works her triceps (B).

Your goal is to work up to completing 10 Mounted Push-Ups in each hand position, for a total of 30. Once again, a reminder that unlike when you do traditional push-ups, in the Mounted Push-Ups you should use only your arms to move your upper body. As you lower your upper body down, concentrate on engaging your arm muscles only, while keeping the back and core relaxed. When you push your upper body away from the horse's crest, do not fully extend the elbow. Remember, this is the Cool Down, so the "up-down" of each push-up should be slow and steady.

# Conclusion

Congratulations, you have now completed the entire Equicize sequence! And if you are like most Everyday Riders who have reached this stage in the journey, you might be thinking—*Phew, I'm glad I survived.* But my hope is you are also encouraged to keep going. To receive the full benefit of any exercise program requires commitment and dedication (fig. C1). You can't simply complete the routine once and expect the benefits to stick.

As I stated at the beginning of this book, Equicize is a tool that can be incorporated into your regular program in a number of ways. A rider can't spend all her mounted practice time doing Equicize exercises and also make progress toward developing other essential skills. But by intersecting Equicize with skill-focused training time, she is likely to see her progress accelerate in both areas.

In Appendix B (p. 145), I have prepared three Equicize Lite Combos. In each combo, there are just four exercises: one from the mounted warm-up sequence, and one each focused on increasing cardio, building strength, and improving the arms. Having done the entire sequence, you will now recognize that every Equicize exercise is also going to challenge your balance, strength, and coordination—even if these qualities are not the specific focus of that

C.1 | **The full benefit of your Equicize program requires commitment and dedication.**

particular exercise. Equicize Lite is designed to fit into the first moments of your ride, leaving the rest of your training time free to practice other skills.

Alternatively, Everyday Riders can pick and choose, selecting those Equicize exercises best targeting those areas of their body most in need of improvement. If you choose this approach, be mindful that you don't only practice those exercises that come easily to you. All riders have their favorite Equicize exercises, but it is equally (or perhaps more) important to practice those exercises you find challenging as well.

Riders seeking to truly progress through the Equicize challenge levels, culminating with the ability to perform the entire sequence in the two-point, at the trot, with few walk breaks, will likely need to dedicate one or two rides per week to completing the full sequence (fig. C2).

While there are always some Everyday Riders who prefer to practice Equicize on their own, over and over, I have seen that those who gather as a group derive

C.2 | **Riders seeking to truly progress through the Equicize challenge levels will likely need to dedicate one or two rides per week to completing the full sequence. Amanda works through her sequence, which includes the Two-Point to Chest Press.**

**C.3 | Remember to log your progress and store it in your tack trunk. Record the number of repetitions and circuits you complete for each exercise and how you felt afterward.**

additional benefits from the experience. The camaraderie of the group helps to motivate its members to push to their personal edge, and keeps them coming back, even when Equicize becomes challenging. As I have introduced Equicize to riders and their trainers across the country, I always encourage them to establish dedicated Equicize sessions, one to three times per week, so they too can enjoy the benefits of a social, supportive group.

Remember to log your progress in a journal and store it in your tack box or locker. Record the number of repetitions and circuits you completed of each exercise, the gait you practiced them in, and how you felt afterward (fig. C3). On the days when Equicize feels especially hard, look back at that log—and see how far you have come.

Of course, I can't tell you exactly how quickly you will notice an improvement in your fitness, or a greater ease in your mounted work. What I can tell you is that every rider who has committed to her Equicize practice in a consistent way has, over time, improved. Riders report feeling stronger and better balanced, being less winded after practicing their usual exercises, and feeling less soreness in the days after their workout. All of this translates into greater proficiency in the saddle, and happier, more successful horse-and-rider partnerships (figs. C4 A & B).

Finally, Equicize may have been my idea, but I want it now to belong to all of you. As you practice, perhaps you will come up with your own variations on exercises, or even create new ones. When you do, I want to hear about it, so I can share your wisdom and experience with Equicizers everywhere.

C.4 A & B | Equicize riders report feeling stronger and better balanced, which lead to happier and more successful horse-and-rider partnerships. Riders at Turning Point Show Stables include (left to right) Marybeth, Stephanie, Loretta, and Megan. Riders at Floyd Woods Stable include (left to right) Reina, Marianne, Morgan, and Amanda.

Author Sally Batton

# About the Authors

**Sally Batton** was the head coach of the Dartmouth College Division I Varsity Equestrian Team for 30 years, coaching dozens of riders to regional, zone, and national titles. In 2020, Coach Batton was inducted into the inaugural class of the Intercollegiate Horse Shows Association Hall of Fame. She currently travels all over the United States, including Alaska and Hawaii, teaching clinics to riders of all ages and levels.

Batton is the author, with co-writer Christina Keim, of *The Athletic Equestrian* (2022, Trafalgar Square). An avid polocrosse enthusiast, Batton is a certified APA Polocrosse Coach, and the author of *Polocrosse: Australian Made, Internationally Played*, (Belcris, 1990).

Batton is the Founder and President of the Athletic Equestrian League, an organization offering horsemanship education and competition opportunities to both English and Western riders, from first grade through adult. She is also the host of the popular Athletic Equestrian Riding in College Podcast.

Batton holds an Equestrian Studies degree from Lake Erie College in Ohio, and a master's degree in Communications from Fairleigh-Dickinson University in New Jersey. An avid hiker and outdoor enthusiast, Batton can be found hiking the hills of New Hampshire, kayaking in the summers, and skiing and snowshoeing in the winter.

**Christina Keim, M. Ed., M.F.A.,** is an award-winning narrative journalist with over one thousand published articles to her credit. Her work has appeared in *The Chronicle of the Horse, UnTacked, Equine Journal, Practical Horseman, The Eastern Equerry, Northeast Equestrian Life, Green Mountain Horse Association Magazine, Woodstock Magazine* and *The Plaid Horse*, among others. With Sally Batton, she is the co-writer of *The Athletic Equestrian* (2022, Trafalgar Square). For nearly two decades a top intercollegiate hunter seat coach, Keim now teaches compassionate horsemanship and offers equine-assisted coaching out of her Cold Moon Farm in Rochester, N.H.

# The Full Equicize Sequence

For your convenience, I have compiled the full Equicize sequence here. Take a picture with your phone, or even snip this page out of the book, for a handy ringside reference!

## Unmounted Warm-Up: Grooming Stretches  p. 38

- Grooming Box Lunge  p. 39
- Curry Comb Toe Raises  p. 41
- Quadriceps Stretch  p. 42
- Lead Rope Shoulder Stretch and Squat  p. 46
- Soft Brush Squats  p. 49
- Achilles Stretch  p. 51
- Whole Body Stretch  p. 53

## Mounted Equicize Warm-Up  p. 64

- Mounted Torso Twist (once to the outside, each direction)  p. 66
- Hip-Forward Pencil Stand (begin with holding for count of five, working up to holding for full circuit)  p. 69
- Sit-Ones (one circuit each of fives, fours, threes, and twos)  p. 73
- Stand-Ones (one circuit each of fives, fours, threes, and twos)  p. 75

## Leg Builders  p. 76

- Two-Point/Chest Press (two circuits of fives, one circuit each of fours, threes, and twos)  p. 77
- One-Handed Chest Press (one full circuit in each direction, stretching to inside only)  p. 81

## Balance Challenges  p. 89

- Pommel Stands on an Increasing Count (one circuit each of twos, threes, fours, and fives)  p. 91
- Two-Point Toe Touches (10 touches in each direction, reaching to inside only)  p. 93

# APPENDIX B:
# Equicize Lite

Obviously, increasing rider fitness is only one component of the many skills and attributes riders need to develop to reach their equestrian goals. For maximum benefit, I recommend that Everyday Riders complete the entire Equicize sequence at least once per week. On those days, Equicize will likely be the only activity on their  mounted agenda.

But the rest of the week, when Everyday Riders are practicing other essential skills, they can still complete a compressed version of the workout in the form of *Equicize Lite*. Each *Equicize Lite* variation includes exercises to help riders warm up, as well as boost their cardiovascular output and build strength. Think of these like an Equicize sampler platter—*Equicize Lite* includes just a few of your favorites, giving Everyday Riders enough of a workout to feel they have accomplished something, while leaving enough energy in their bodies and time in their ride to continue pursuing additional goals.

In each of these *Equicize Lite Combos*, Everyday Riders should plan to complete the same number of repetitions, and the same count, as in the full work out.

## Equicize Lite Combo # 1

### Warm-Up
- Mounted Torso Twist (Twist once to the outside in each direction—p. 66)
- Stand-Ones (one circuit each of fives, fours, threes, and twos—p. 75)

### Cardio
- Pommel Stands on an Increasing Count (one circuit each of twos, threes, fours, and fives—p. 91)

### Strength
- Gluteal Squeezes (two circuits, holding for 10 count, resting for 10 count—p. 121)

***Arms***

- Popeye and Under-Arm Popeye (10 repetitions of each exercise on each arm—pp. 103 and 107)

## Equicize Lite Combo #2

***Warm-Up***

- Sit-Ones (one circuit each of fives, fours, threes, and twos—p. 73)

***Cardio***

- Two-Point/Chest Press (two circuits of fives, one circuit each of fours, threes, and twos—p. 77)

***Strength***

- Abdominal Squeezes (two circuits, holding for 10 count, resting for 10 count—p. 121)

***Arms***

- Stop Sign and Chicken Wing (10 repetitions of each exercise on each arm—pp. 108 and 111)

## Equicize Lite Combo #3

***Warm-up***

- Stand-Ones (one circuit each of fives, fours, threes, and twos—p. 75)

***Cardio***

- One-Handed Chest Press (one full circuit in each direction, stretching to inside only—p. 81)

***Strength***

- Two-Point Toe Touches (10 touches in each direction, reaching to inside only—p. 93)

***Arms***

- Boxer Punches and Victory Punches (10 repetitions of each exercise on each arm—pp. 113 and 115)

# Equicize Award Checklist

Equicize is a rider-fitness system that provides challenge to Everyday Riders at all levels of fitness. By modifying each exercise to help her find her personal edge, an Equicizer can work to progressively increase her flexibility, strength, balance, and coordination in the saddle.

One of the biggest challenges Everyday Riders can face along their road to personal fitness is staying motivated over time. It is completely normal for athletes to find that their path to fitness is not linear; instead, there are periods of ease, and periods of challenge. Equicizing with friends, to music, can help many rider-athletes through some of the challenging phases of their journey. But for some riders, a more tangible goal is helpful.

Here in Appendix C, you will find three checklists, corresponding with the Equicize Bronze, Silver, and Gold Awards. As Equicizers gain fitness, these checklists provide three tangible benchmarks to strive toward in their workouts. Once an Equicizer completes all the tasks on each checklist, she will earn the corresponding award.

Ultimately, the Equicize Awards are honor-system based. I am not going to travel to your barn, or require you to send a video, "proving" to me or anyone else that you can do the exercises as listed. Instead, look to these lists as long-term goals, and just as you have done for every other component of the Equicize program, listen to your body, and modify accordingly. We are all individuals, with unique physical needs. Your own personal Bronze, Silver, and Gold levels may look a little bit different than exactly what is listed here. The goal is to find your personal edge, then push it—ever so gently—just a little farther.

Once achieved, Equicizers can order their Equicize Awards from Equicize.com.

# BRONZE EQUICIZE AWARD

*Perform all of the exercises
below at the walk*

- ☐ SIT-ONES
- ☐ STAND-ONES
- ☐ POMMEL STANDS
- ☐ GLUTE SQUEEZES
- ☐ ABS SQUEEZES
- ☐ TWO-PT TO CHEST PRESS
- ☐ TWO-PT TOE TOUCHES
- ☐ ONE-HANDED CHEST PRESS
- ☐ POPEYE
- ☐ UNDER-ARM POPEYE
- ☐ STOP SIGN
- ☐ CHICKEN WING
- ☐ BOXER PUNCHES
- ☐ VICTORY PUNCHES
- ☐ PUSH-UPS

# SILVER EQUICIZE AWARD

*Perform all of the exercises
below at the trot*

- ☐ SIT-ONES
- ☐ STAND-ONES
- ☐ POMMEL STANDS
- ☐ GLUTE SQUEEZES
- ☐ ABS SQUEEZES
- ☐ TWO-PT TO CHEST PRESS
- ☐ TWO-PT TOE TOUCHES
- ☐ ONE-HANDED CHEST PRESS
- ☐ POPEYE
- ☐ UNDER-ARM POPEYE
- ☐ STOP SIGN
- ☐ CHICKEN WING
- ☐ BOXER PUNCHES
- ☐ VICTORY PUNCHES
- ☐ PUSH-UPS

# GOLD EQUICIZE AWARD

*Perform all of the exercises
below at the trot with
no stirrups*

- ☐ SIT-ONES
- ☐ STAND-ONES
- ☐ POMMEL STANDS
- ☐ GLUTE SQUEEZES
- ☐ ABS SQUEEZES
- ☐ TWO-PT TO CHEST PRESS
- ☐ TWO-PT TOE TOUCHES
- ☐ ONE-HANDED CHEST PRESS
- ☐ POPEYE
- ☐ UNDER-ARM POPEYE
- ☐ STOP SIGN
- ☐ CHICKEN WING
- ☐ BOXER PUNCHES
- ☐ VICTORY PUNCHES
- ☐ PUSH-UPS

# ATHLETIC EQUESTRIAN AND EQUICIZE:
# Learn More!

Learn more about Equicize and everything that Sally Batton has to offer through Athletic Equestrian! Book a clinic with Sally or one of her Certified Equicize Coaches at www.equicize.com.

Sally travels all over the United States and internationally to teach clinics to correct common position faults on the flat and over fences based on her book *The Athletic Equestrian*. All ages and abilities will benefit from Sally's attentive and positive teaching style.

You can also join her on her podcast Athletic Equestrian Riding in College where she interviews collegiate coaches, riders, and organizations for their insight on what it takes to ride on a collegiate equestrian team and beyond! Available on Spotify and Apple Podcasts.

**www.athleticequestrian.com**
**athleticequestrian@gmail.com**

# Acknowledgments

*quicize* has been 30 years in the making and I have many people to thank for bringing it to life. I had this idea of a mounted workout program back when I was not only coaching the Dartmouth College Equestrian Team but also teaching community adult riding classes at Dartmouth Riding Center in Etna, New Hampshire. My fellow riding instructor and long-time friend Lori Wakeman and I started experimenting with putting our fitness class workouts onto horseback. So deep gratitude to Lori for those original moves and her support and friendship through all these years!

Thank you to my trusty co-writer and friend Christina Keim who listened to my stream of consciousness on our chapter conference calls and put them into the beautiful and entertaining words that explain Equicize so well. Thanks to my photographer Ashley Yeaton and my videographer Worthy Gardner, who were both so patient with my giant lists for each and every shoot. Thank you to my wonderful riders who did take after take to get the right shots: Megan, Marybeth, Loretta, and Stephanie at Turning Point Show Stables in E. Kingston, New Hampshire; Reina, Morgan, Amanda, and Marianne at Floyd Woods Farm in Lempster, New Hampshire; and Tami, Edie, and Madison at Wakewood Farm in Plymouth, New Hampshire. Thank you to my beta readers Cara McSoley, Kim Kerschl, and Suzanne McGovern who read through the final draft for content and clarity.

A very special thank you to my children, Emma, Jenna, and Jack, to whom I dedicate this book. Through the years their love and support has been my inspiration and I am so proud of the spectacular adults they have become. Thank you to my husband Ed for his love and patience with my absences, not only away teaching clinics but for the hours and days I spent holed up in my office working on my books.

And finally, a profound thank you to my publishers Trafalgar Square Books, especially to Martha Cook and Rebecca Didier, for their patience with my hundreds of questions and their guidance through our books from start to finish.

# Index

## Severity of Psychosocial Stressors Scale: Children and Adolescents

See p. 33 for instructions on how to use this scale.

| Code | Term | Examples of stressors | |
|---|---|---|---|
| | | Acute events | Enduring circumstances |
| 1 | None | No acute events that may be relevant to the disorder | No enduring circumstances that may be relevant to the disorder |
| 2 | Mild | Broke up with boyfriend or girlfriend; change of school | Overcrowded living quarters; family arguments |
| 3 | Moderate | Expelled from school; birth of sibling | Chronic disabling illness in parent; chronic parental discord |
| 4 | Severe | Divorce of parents; unwanted pregnancy; arrest | Harsh or rejecting parents; chronic life-threatening illness in parent; multiple foster home placements |
| 5 | Extreme | Sexual or physical abuse; death of a parent | Recurrent sexual or physical abuse |
| 6 | Catastrophic | Death of both parents | Chronic life-threatening illness |
| 0 | Inadequate information, or no change in condition | | |

## Global Assessment of Functioning Scale (GAF Scale)

Consider psychological, social, and occupational functioning on a hypothetical continuum of mental health–illness. Do not include impairment in functioning due to physical (or environmental) limitations. See p. 37 for instructions on how to use this scale.

**Note:** Use intermediate codes when appropriate, e.g., 45, 68, 72.

**Code**

90
    **Absent or minimal symptoms** (e.g., mild anxiety before an exam), **good functioning in all areas, interested and involved in a wide range of activities, socially effective, generally satisfied with life, no more than everyday problems or concerns** (e.g., an occasional argument with family members).
81

80
    **If symptoms are present, they are transient and expectable reactions to psychosocial stressors** (e.g., difficulty concentrating after family argument); **no more than slight impairment in social, occupational, or school functioning** (e.g., temporarily falling behind in school work).
71

70
    **Some mild symptoms** (e.g., depressed mood and mild insomnia) **OR some difficulty in social, occupational, or school functioning** (e.g., occasional truancy, or theft within the household), **but generally functioning pretty well, has some meaningful interpersonal relationships.**
61

60
    **Moderate symptoms** (e.g., flat affect and circumstantial speech, occasional panic attacks) **OR moderate difficulty in social, occupational, or school functioning** (e.g., few friends, conflicts with co-workers).
51

| 50 | **Serious symptoms** (e.g., suicidal ideation, severe obsessional rituals, frequent shoplifting) **OR any serious impairment in social, occupational, or school functioning** (e.g., no friends, unable to keep a job). |
| 41 | |
| 40 | **Some impairment in reality testing or communication** (e.g., speech is at times illogical, obscure, or irrelevant) **OR major impairment in several areas, such as work or school, family relations, judgment, thinking, or mood** (e.g., depressed man avoids friends, neglects family, and is unable to work; child frequently beats up younger children, is defiant at home, and is failing at school). |
| 31 | |
| 30 | **Behavior is considerably influenced by delusions or hallucinations OR serious impairment in communication or judgment** (e.g., sometimes incoherent, acts grossly inappropriately, suicidal preoccupation) **OR inability to function in almost all areas** (e.g., stays in bed all day; no job, home, or friends). |
| 21 | |
| 20 | **Some danger of hurting self or others** (e.g., suicide attempts without clear expectation of death, frequently violent, manic excitement) **OR occasionally fails to maintain minimal personal hygiene** (e.g., smears feces) **OR gross impairment in communication** (e.g., largely incoherent or mute). |
| 11 | |
| 10 | **Persistent danger of severely hurting self or others** (e.g., recurrent violence) **OR persistent inability to maintain minimal personal hygiene OR serious suicidal act with clear expectation of death.** |
| 1 | |

# Use of This Manual

# Use of This Manual

This chapter includes a discussion of the following:



## MULTIAXIAL EVALUATION

A multiaxial evaluation requires that every case be assessed on several "axes," each of which refers to a different class of information. In order for the system to have maximal clinical usefulness, there must be a limited number of axes; there are five in the DSM-III-R multiaxial classification. The first three axes constitute the official diagnostic assessment.

Use of the DSM-III-R multiaxial system ensures that attention is given to certain types of disorders, aspects of the environment, and areas of functioning that might be overlooked if the focus were on assessing a single presenting problem. Each person is evaluated on each of these axes:

Axis I      Clinical Syndromes and V Codes
Axis II     Developmental Disorders and Personality
            Disorders
Axis III    Physical Disorders and Conditions
Axis IV     Severity of Psychosocial Stressors
Axis V      Global Assessment of Functioning

Axes IV and V are available for use in special clinical and research settings; they provide information that supplements the official DSM-III-R diagnoses (on Axes I, II, and III) and that may be useful for planning treatment and predicting outcome.

## Axes I and II. Mental Disorders and V Codes

Axes I and II constitute the entire classification of mental disorders plus V Codes (Conditions Not Attributable to a Mental Disorder That Are a Focus of Attention or Treatment). The disorders listed on Axis II, Developmental Disorders and Personality Disorders, generally begin in childhood or adolescence and persist in a stable form (without periods of remission or exacerbation) into adult life. With only a few exceptions (e.g., the Gender Identity Disorders and Paraphilias), these features are not characteristic of the Axis I disorders. The separation between Axis I and Axis II ensures that in the evaluation of adults, consideration is given to the possible presence of Personality Disorders that may be overlooked when attention is directed to the usually more florid Axis I disorder. The Axis I–Axis II distinction in evaluating children emphasizes the need to consider disorders involving the development of cognitive, social, and motor skills.

In many instances there will be a disorder on both axes. For example, an adult may have Major Depression noted on Axis I and Obsessive Compulsive Personality Disorder on Axis II, or a child may have Conduct Disorder noted on Axis I and Developmental Language Disorder on Axis II. In other instances there may be no disorder on Axis I, the reason for seeking treatment being limited to a condition noted on Axis II. In this latter case, the clinician should write: *Axis I:* V71.09 No diagnosis or condition on Axis I, or one of the Conditions Not Attributable to a Mental Disorder should be recorded. On the other hand, if a disorder is noted on Axis I but there is no evidence of an Axis II disorder, the clinician should write: *Axis II:* V71.09 No diagnosis on Axis II.

## Multiple diagnoses within Axes I and II

On both Axes I and II, multiple diagnoses should be made when necessary to describe the current condition. This applies particularly to Axis I, on which, for example, a person may have both a Psychoactive Substance Use Disorder and a Mood Disorder. It is also possible to have multiple diagnoses within the same class. For example, it is possible to have several Psychoactive Substance Use Disorders or, in the class of Mood Disorders, it is possible to have Major Depression superimposed on Dysthymia or Bipolar Disorder superimposed on Cyclothymia. In other classes, such as Schizophrenia, however, each of the types is mutually exclusive.

Within Axis II, the diagnosis of multiple Specific Developmental Disorders is common. For some adults the persistence of a Specific Developmental Disorder and the presence of a Personality Disorder may require that both be noted on Axis II. Usually, a single Personality Disorder will be noted; but when the person meets the criteria for more than one, all should be recorded.

## Axis II and description of personality features

Axis II can be used to indicate specific personality traits or the habitual use of particular defense mechanisms (see Glossary for definitions). This can be done when no Personality Disorder exists or to supplement a Personality Disorder diagnosis. (Code numbers are not used when personality traits are noted, since a code number indicates a Personality Disorder.)

*Examples:*

Axis II: 301.40   Obsessive Compulsive Personality
                  Disorder with paranoid traits
Axis II: V71.09   No diagnosis on Axis II but massive
                  denial of Axis III disorder (juvenile
                  diabetes)

## Principal diagnosis

When a person receives more than one diagnosis, the *principal* diagnosis is the condition that was chiefly responsible for occasioning the evaluation or admission to clinical care. In most cases this condition will